MRS. LEICESTER'S SCHOOL

MRS. LEICESTER'S SCHOOL

by

CHARLES & MARY LAMB

1948

LONDON: THE HARVILL PRESS LIMITED

PUBLISHED BY
THE HARVILL PRESS LIMITED
23 LOWER BELGRAVE STREET
LONDON, S.W.I
PRINTED IN GREAT BRITAIN BY
JAMES WILKES LTD.
BILSTON STAFFS.

CONTENTS

* The tales marked with an asterisk are by Charles Lamb; the others by his sister Mary.

Introduction

IN a letter written to his friend Manning in the Far East, under the date 5th December, 1806, Charles Lamb says "Those *Tales from Shakespeare* are near coming out, and Mary has begun a new work." That is the first hint of the genesis of the little collection of anecdotes which grew into a book for children, to be published in 1808 under the title of *Mrs. Leicester's School*.

The little book of ten tales, which the reader will now be able to peruse as it were in the light of a St. Martin's summer of appreciation, pleased not only the children of the early nineteenth century. Listen to what Samuel Taylor Coleridge, that garrulous giant, said of it.

"It at once soothes and amuses me to think—nay, to know—that the time will come when this little volume of my dear and well-nigh oldest friend, Mary Lamb, will be not only enjoyed but acknowledged as a rich jewel in the treasury of our permanent English literature; and I cannot help running over in my mind the long list of celebrated writers, astonishing geniuses, Novels, Romances, Poems,

Histories and dense Political Economy quartos, which, compared with Mrs. Leicester's School, will, be remembered as often and praised as highly as Wilkie's and Glover's Epics and Lord Bolingbroke's Philosophies compared with Robinson Crusoe!"

That is a blurb which any publisher would take as a treasure for the dust jacket. It might well serve as the best introduction to these little moral homilies, and through them to the character and genius of Mary Lamb. The world knows her story. It is a sad, desperate one, a tale with no resolution, with no tragic significance. Here was a woman of complete unselfishness and remarkable talent. She had a great capacity for love and service. These qualities she shared with her brother. Yet both of them were cursed with a certain instability of mind. It led Charles to many dark intervals, many acts of frustration and periods of agonising inaction, it led Mary to an act of insanity. The rest of their domestic story is told in a sort of twilight. Until his death nearly forty years later, Charles devoted himself to the guardianship of this sister whom he loved so tenderly. Her influence on his life was one of gentleness. In the intervals of bouts of mental storm, Mary carried on, at least in the early and more impoverished years of the ménage, her quiet craft of mantua-maker. We can picture them sitting together in their rooms in Clerkenwell, and later in the Temple, during the evenings when the

India House clerk was not in the company of his literary friends. She would be sitting beside the lamp, with the needle flashing in her hand. He would be reading, silent at times, and at others sharing a passage of prose or verse with her, forgetting to stutter under the animation of his enthusiasm.

As they joined in such periods of leisure, so they also collaborated in these occasional little books for children, one book of which is world-famous. The *Tales from Shakespeare* is a standard school prize, and has been so for over a century. *Mrs. Leicester's School* has long been out of print. Of its ten pieces only three are by Charles, and they are inferior to the others written by Mary. They are inferior because, as tales written expressly for children, they lack movement, are much too subjective in texture to command a child's attention, and they contain too many references to books. Further, Charles' sentences are often clumsy, as though, in his effort to make Elia stoop to address children, he has induced a cramp into the limbs of his usually agile mind. Look, for instance, at this limping sentence describing the gargoyles on the Temple Church (monsters familiar to him from his own infant days). "My Father said they were very improper ornaments for such a place, and so I now think them; but it seems the people who built these great churches in old times gave themselves more liberties than they do now; and I remember that when I first saw them, and before my father had made this observation, though they were so ugly and out of shape, and some of them seemed to be grinning and distorting their features with pain or with laughter, yet being placed upon a church, to which I had come with such serious thoughts, I could not help thinking they had some serious meaning; and I looked at them with wonder, but without any temptation to laugh." By the time that sentence is ended, I fear, the child asked to look at the gargoyles will have fallen asleep on Oliver Goldsmith's monument, which is nearby (or was nearby, before the Temple fell).

I am, however, unhistorical in picturing Elia trying to stoop to child-height; for in fact Elia was not born (and what a second birth that was!) until 1820, twelve years after *Mrs. Leicester's School* was published. Lamb began his first essays under that name in the newly founded London Magazine. At the time of his collaboration with his sister Mary, Charles was not inexperienced in the difficult art of writing for children. One might even say that *Rosamund Gray*, that classic novelette, could be offered for puerile reading, and offered with some success, for the story, in spite of its horror (and what child is repelled by horror?) is told with great simplicity and directness. Lamb has also written for children under the title "The King and Queen of Hearts: showing how notably the Queen made her Tarts, and how scurvily the Knave stole them away:

with other particulars pertaining thereto." This effort was issued anonymously, and disappeared for a century before being discovered and accredited to its author. It consisted of a number of pictures, each subscribed with some lines of verse written in the manner of the first Samuel Butler, the author of Hudibras. After that, Mary took a hand in her young brother's essays to amuse the nursery, and the first fruit of this collaboration was the *Tales from Shakespeare*, which introduced the authors to William Godwin, the philosopher-sponger-publisher, and his notorious wife, at their premises in Skinner Street where Shelley met Mary Godwin, and no doubt where Lamb encountered the aristocratic poet and took an instant dislike to him and his shrill voice.

Mary shared with her brother the possession of genius. The first few sentences of *Mrs. Leicester's School* proclaim it. Knowing the capital difficulty of achieving simplicity, I marvel at the ease of her writing, and the transparency of it. In these two qualities I must compare her to the authors of *The Vicar of Wakefield* and *Manon Lescaut*. In her seven tales, she writes in the first person, through the minds of seven small girls who are gathered round their mistress on their first night at a new school. By means of each telling the story of her life, the girls are made of a more fluid acquaintance with each other, the ice of the first night at school is broken. Their relation of events is small enough. There is no high drama. But how much human consciousness Mary can put *behind* the narrative; what a background of pathos and tenderness, and what a formidable ridge of irony. Walter Savage Landor, coming later on the little book, remarked that one sentence in *The Father's Wedding Night* was worth the whole of Richardson's *Clarissa* and Rousseau's *Heloise*. The sentence occurs on page 65. To take its full burden of pathos, one has to have the atmosphere of the tale, with the skilfully inferred characters of the dead mother with her poor head and her ravaged face against the mass of cushions, the vivid eyes of the new step-mother, and the abrupt, clumsy nature of the father. And all this creation of character is done by inference, through the naïve words of a child. How arch, how falsely simple, it might have been. But Mary Lamb makes it honest, inevitable, almost classical in its starkness. The child is dressed in her finery for the wedding of her father to this stranger whom she has not yet seen. She is so proud of the dress that she goes, as has always been her habit, to the mat outside the bedroom door of her dead mother. "When I was dressed in my new frock, I wished poor mamma was alive to see how fine I was on papa's wedding day, and I ran to my favourite station at her bedroom door." A. E. Housman, that sardonic curmudgeon with a golden Latin tongue, could not be more excoriating in his poem

Is Football Playing. That is one of the subtle touches which make these tales so memorable. I hardly need to point to others: the quick limning of character by oblique suggestion; the humour; the choice of epithet which at times is Miltonic, as where the dust-covers in an unused room full of treasures are described as "the envious cloth."

Few people today, either adult or young, have heard of *Mrs. Leicester's School.* Yet it was successful when it appeared. Ten editions were put out by the impecunious Godwins during the lifetime of the authors: and it is to be hoped that they profited a little by the success. It is improbable, for the incapacity of Godwin and the rapacity of his wife would have combined to build a high dam against the overflow of any royalties from that publishing house, if indeed the payment of royalties were ever undertaken by it.

The general impression made by the book leads to some useful meditation upon the changes which have taken place in the circumstances, the moral and cultural environment, amid which upper middle-class children are brought up today, as compared with those of a century ago. I will not suggest what conclusions may be drawn from that meditation; but it may be hinted that difference, rather than progression, is the word to describe these changes.

RICHARD CHURCH.

MRS. LEICESTER'S SCHOOL

OR

THE HISTORY OF SEVERAL YOUNG LADIES

RELATED BY THEMSELVES.

Dedication.

TO THE
YOUNG LADIES AT AMWELL SCHOOL.

MY DEAR YOUNG FRIENDS,—Though released from the business of the school, the absence of your governess confines me to Amwell during the vacation. I cannot better employ my leisure hours than in contributing to the amusement of you, my kind pupils, who, by your affectionate attentions to my instructions, have rendered a life of labour pleasant to me.

On your return to school I hope to have a fair copy, ready to present to each of you, of your own biographical conversations last winter.

Accept my thanks for the approbation you were pleased to express when I offered to become your amanuensis. I hope you will find I have executed the office with a tolerably faithful pen, as you know I took notes each day during those conversations, and arranged my materials after you were retired to rest.

I begin from the day our school commenced. It was opened by your governess for the first time on the——day of February. I pass over your several arrivals on the morning of that day. Your governess received you from your friends in her own parlour.

Every carriage that drove from the door I knew had left a sad heart behind. Your eyes were red with weeping, when your governess introduced me to you as the teacher she had engaged to instruct you. She next desired me to show you into the room which we now call the playroom. "The ladies," said she, "may play and amuse themselves, and be as happy as they please this evening, that they may be well acquainted with each other before they enter the schoolroom to-morrow morning."

The traces of tears were on every cheek, and I also was sad; for I, like you, had parted from my friends, and the duties of my profession were new to me, yet I felt that it was improper to give way to my own melancholy thoughts. I knew that it was my first duty to divert the solitary young strangers; for I considered that this was very unlike the entrance to an old-established school, where there is always some good-natured girl who will show attentions to a new scholar, and take pleasure in initiating her into the customs and amusements of the place. These, thought I, have their own amusements to invent;

2

their own customs to establish. How unlike, too, is this forlorn meeting to old schoolfellows returning after the holidays, when mutual greetings soon lighten the memory of parting sorrow.

I invited you to draw near a bright fire which blazed in the chimney, and looked the only cheerful thing in the room.

During our first solemn silence, which, you may remember, was only broken by my repeated requests that you would make a smaller and still smaller circle, till I saw the fireplace fairly enclosed round, the idea came into my mind, which has since been a source of amusement to you in the recollection, and to myself in particular has been of essential benefit, as it enabled me to form a just estimate of the dispositions of you, my young pupils, and assisted me to adopt my plan of future instructions to each individual temper.

An introduction to a point we wish to carry, we always feel to be an awkward affair, and generally execute it in an awkward manner; so I believe I did then; for when I imparted this idea to you, I think I prefaced it rather too formally for such young auditors; for I began with telling you that I had read in old authors, that it was not unfrequent in former times, when strangers were assembled together, as we might be, for them to amuse themselves with telling stories—either of their own lives, or the adventures of others. "Will you allow me, ladies," I continued, "to persuade you to amuse yourselves in this way? You will not then look so unsociably upon each other; for we find that these strangers, of whom we read, were as well acquainted before the conclusion of the first story as if they had known each other many years. Let me prevail upon you to relate some little anecdotes of your own lives. Fictitious tales we can read in books, and they were therefore better adapted to conversation in those times when books of amusement were more scarce than they are at present."

After many objections of not knowing what to say or how to begin, which I overcame by assuring you how easy it would be, for that every person is naturally eloquent when they are the hero or heroine of their own tale;—the *Who should begin?* was next in question.

I proposed to draw lots, which formed a little amusement of itself. Miss Manners, who till then had been the saddest of the sad, began to brighten, and said it was just like drawing king and queen; and began to tell us where she passed last Twelfth-day; but as her narration must have interfered with the more important business of the lottery, I advised her to postpone it till it came to her turn to favour us with the history of her life, when it would appear in its proper order. The first number fell to the share of Miss Villiers, whose joy at drawing what we called the *first prize* was tempered with shame at appearing as the first historian in the company. She wished she had not been the very first:—she had passed all her life in a retired village, and had nothing to relate of herself that could give the least entertainment; she had not the least idea in the world where to begin.

"Begin," said I, "with your name, for that at present is unknown to us. Tell us the first thing you can remember; relate whatever happened to make a great impression on you when you were very young; and if you find you can connect your story till your arrival here to-day, I am sure we shall listen to you with pleasure; and if you like to break off, and only treat us with a part of your history, we will excuse you, with many thanks for the amusement which you have afforded us; and the young lady who has drawn the second number will, I hope, take her turn with the same indulgence, to relate either all, or any part of the events of her life, as best pleases her own fancy, or as she finds she can manage it with the most ease to herself." Encouraged by this offer of indulgence, Miss Villiers began.

If in my report of her story, or in any which follow, I shall appear to make her or you speak an older language than it seems probable that you should use, speaking in your own words, it must be remembered that what is very proper and becoming when spoken, requires to be arranged with some little difference before it can be set down in writing. Little inaccuracies must be pared away, and the whole must assume a more formal and correct appearance.

My own way of thinking, I am sensible, will too often intrude itself; but I have endeavoured to preserve, as exactly as I could, your own words and your own peculiarities of style and manner, and to approve myself.

Your faithful historiographer,

as well as true friend,

M. B.

Elizabeth Villiers

THE SAILOR UNCLE

M Y father is the curate of a village church about five miles from Amwell. I was born in the parsonage-house, which joins the churchyard. The first thing I can remember was my father teaching me the alphabet from the letters on a tombstone that stood at the head of my mother's grave. I used to tap at my father's study door; I think I now hear him say, "Who is there?—What do you want, little girl?" "Go and see mamma. Go and learn pretty letters." Many times in the day would my father lay aside his books and his papers to lead me to this spot, and make me point to the letters, and then set me to spell syllables and words: in this manner, the epitaph on my mother's tomb being my primer and my spelling-book, I learned to read.

I was one day sitting on a step placed across the churchyard stile, when a gentleman, passing by, heard me distinctly repeat the letters which formed my mother's name, and then say *Elizabeth Villiers*, with a firm tone, as if I had performed some great matter. This gentleman was my uncle James, my mother's brother; he was a lieutenant in the Navy,

7

and had left England a few weeks after the marriage of my father and mother, and now, returned home from a long sea-voyage, he was coming to visit my mother—no tidings of her decease having reached him, though she had been dead more than a twelve-month.

When my uncle saw me sitting on the stile, and heard me pronounce my mother's name, he looked earnestly in my face, and began to fancy a resemblance to his sister, and to think I might be her child. I was too intent on my employment to observe him, and went spelling on. "Who has taught you to spell so prettily, my little maid?" said my uncle. "Mamma," I replied; for I had an idea that the words on the tombstone were somehow a part of mamma, and that she had taught me. "And who is mamma?" asked my uncle. "Elizabeth Villiers," I replied; and then my uncle called me his dear little niece, and said he would go with me to mamma; he took hold of my hand, intending to lead me home, delighted that he had found out who I was, because he imagined it would be such a pleasant surprise to his sister to see her little daughter bringing home her long-lost sailor uncle.

I agreed to take him to mamma, but we had a dispute about the way thither. My uncle was for going along the road which led directly up to our house; I pointed to the churchyard, and said that was the way to mamma. Though impatient of any

8

delay, he was not willing to contest the point with his new relation; therefore he lifted me over the stile, and was then going to take me along the path to a gate he knew was at the end of our garden; but no, I would not go that way neither; letting go his hand, I said, "You do not know the way,—I will show you;" and making what haste I could among the long grass and thistles, and jumping over the low graves, he said, as he followed what he called my *wayward steps*, "What a positive soul this little niece of mine is! I knew the way to your mother's house before you were born, child." At last I stopped at my mother's grave, and pointing to the tombstone said, "Here is mamma!" in a voice of exultation, as if I had now convinced him that I knew the way best. I looked up in his face to see him acknowledge his mistake; but oh! what a face of sorrow did I see! I was so frightened, that I have but an imperfect recollection of what followed. I remember I pulled his coat, and cried "Sir, sir!" and tried to move him. I knew not what to do. My mind was in a strange confusion; I thought I had done something wrong in bringing the gentleman to mamma, to make him cry so sadly; but what it was I could not tell. This grave had always been a scene of delight to me. In the house my father would often be weary of my prattle, and send me from him; but here he was all my own. I might say anything, and be as frolic-some as I pleased here; all was cheerfulness and

9

good humour in our visits to mamma, as we called it. My father would tell me how quietly mamma slept there, and that he and his little Betsy would one day sleep beside mamma in that grave; and when I went to bed, as I laid my little head on the pillow, I used to wish I was sleeping in the grave with papa and mamma; and in my childish dreams I used to fancy myself there; and it was a place within the ground, all smooth, and soft, and green. I never made out any figure of mamma, but still it was the tombstone, and papa, and the smooth green grass, and my head resting upon the elbow of my father.

How long my uncle remained in this agony of grief I know not—to me it seemed a very long time; at last he took me in his arms, and held me so tight that I began to cry, and ran home to my father and told him that a gentleman was crying about mamma's pretty letters.

No doubt it was a very affecting meeting between my father and uncle. I remember that it was the very first day I ever saw my father weep—that I was in sad trouble, and went into the kitchen and told Susan, our servant, that papa was crying; and she wanted to keep me with her, that I might not disturb the conversation; but I would go back to the parlour to *poor papa*, and I went in softly and crept between my father's knees. My uncle offered to take me in his arms, but I turned sullenly from him, and clung closer to my father, having conceived a dislike to my uncle because he had made my father cry.

Now I first learned that my mother's death was a heavy affliction; for I heard my father tell a melancholy story of her long illness, her death, and what he had suffered from her loss. My uncle said what a sad thing it was for my father to be left with such a young child; but my father replied, his little Betsy was all his comfort, and that, but for me, he should have died with grief. How I could be any comfort to my father, struck me with wonder. I knew I was pleased when he played and talked with me; but I thought that was all goodness and favour done to me, and I had no notion how I could make any part of his happiness. The sorrow I now heard he had suffered was as new and strange to me. I had no idea that he had ever been unhappy; his voice was always kind and cheerful; I had never before seen him weep, or show any signs of grief as those in which I used to express my little troubles. My thoughts on these subjects were confused and childish; but from that time I never ceased pondering on the sad story of my dead mamma.

The next day I went, by mere habit, to the study door, to call papa to the beloved grave; my mind misgave me, and I could not tap on the door. I went backwards and forwards between the kitchen and the study, and what to do with myself I did not know. My uncle met me in the passage, and said, "Betsy, will you come and walk with me in the garden?"

This I refused, for this was not what I wanted, but the old amusement of sitting on the grave and talking to papa. My uncle tried to persuade me, but still I said, "No, no," and ran crying into the kitchen. As he followed me in there, Susan said, "This child is so fretful to-day, I do not know what to do with her." "Ay," said my uncle, "I suppose my poor brother spoils her, having but one." This reflection on my papa made me quite in a little passion of anger, for I had not forgot that with this new uncle sorrow had first come into our dwelling; I screamed loudly, till my father came out to know what it was all about. He sent my uncle into the parlour, and said he would manage the little wrangler by himself. When my uncle was gone I ceased crying; my father forgot to lecture me for my ill-humour, or to inquire into the cause, and we were soon seated by the side of the tombstone. No lesson went on that day; no talking of pretty mamma sleeping in the green grave; no jumping from the tombstone to the ground; no merry jokes or pleasant stories. I sat upon my father's knee, looking up in his face and thinking, "*How sorry papa looks*," till having been fatigued with crying, and now oppressed with thought, I fell fast asleep.

My uncle soon learned from Susan that this place was our constant haunt; she told him she did verily believe her master would never get the better of the death of her mistress while he continued to teach the child to read at the tombstone; for though it might soothe his grief, it kept it for ever fresh in his memory. The sight of his sister's grave had been such a shock to my uncle, that he readily entered into Susan's apprehensions; and concluding that if I were set to study by some other means, there would no longer be a pretence for these visits to the grave, away my kind uncle hastened to the nearest market-town to buy me some books.

I heard the conference between my uncle and Susan, and I did not approve of his interfering in our pleasure. I saw him take his hat and walk out, and I secretly hoped he was gone *beyond seas again*, from whence Susan had told me he had come. Where *beyond seas* was, I could not tell, but I concluded it was somewhere a great way off. I took my seat on the churchyard stile, and kept looking down the road, and saying, "I hope I shall not see my uncle again. I hope my uncle will not come from *beyond seas* any more;" but I said this very softly, and had a kind of notion that I was in a perverse ill-humoured fit. Here I sat till my uncle returned from the market-town with his new purchases. I saw him come walking very fast, with a parcel under his arm. I was very sorry to see him, and I frowned and tried to look very cross. He untied his parcel, and said, "Betsy, I have brought you a pretty book." I turned my head away, and said, "I don't want a book;" but I could not help peeping again to look at it. In the hurry of opening the parcel, he had scattered all the books upon the ground, and there I saw fine gilt covers and gay pictures all fluttering about. What a fine sight! All my resentment vanished, and I held up my face to kiss him, that being my way of thanking my father for any extraordinary favour.

My uncle had brought himself into rather a troublesome office; he had heard me spell so well, that he thought there was nothing to do but to put books into my hand and I should read; yet notwithstanding I spelt tolerably well, the letters in my new library were so much smaller than I had been accustomed to; they were like Greek characters to me; I could make nothing at all of them. The honest sailor was not to be discouraged by this difficulty; though unused to play the schoolmaster, he taught me to read the small print with unwearied diligence and patience; and whenever he saw my father and me look as if we wanted to resume our visits to the grave, he would propose some pleasant walk; and if my father said it was too far for the child to walk, he would set me on his shoulder and say, "Then Betsy shall ride!" and in this manner has he carried me many, many miles.

In these pleasant excursions my uncle seldom forgot to make Susan furnish him with a luncheon, which, though it generally happened every day, made a constant surprise to my papa and me, when, seated under some shady tree, he pulled it out of his pocket, and began to distribute his little store; and then I used to peep into the other pocket, to see if there were not some currant wine there, and the little bottle of water for me; if, perchance, the water was forgot, then it made another joke,—that poor Betsy must be forced to drink a little drop of wine. These are childish things to tell of; and, instead of my own silly history, I wish I could remember the entertaining stories my uncle used to relate of his voyages and travels, while we sat under the shady trees eating our noontide meal.

The long visit my uncle made us was such an important event in my life, that I fear I shall tire your patience with talking of him; but when he is gone, the remainder of my story will be but short.

The summer months passed away, but not swiftly; —the pleasant walks and the charming stories of my uncle's adventures made them seem like years to me. I remember the approach of winter by the warm greatcoat he bought for me, and how proud I was when I first put it on; and that he called me Little Red Riding Hood, and bade me beware of wolves; and that I laughed, and said there were no such things now; then he told me how many wolves, and bears, and tigers, and lions he had met with in uninhabited lands that were like Robinson Crusoe's island. Oh, these were happy days!

In the winter our walks were shorter and less

frequent. My books were now my chief amusement, though my studies were often interrupted by a game of romps with my uncle, which too often ended in a quarrel, because he played so roughly; yet long before this I dearly loved my uncle, and the improvement I made while he was with us was very great indeed. I could now read very well, and the continual habit of listening to the conversation of my father and my uncle made me a little woman in understanding; so that my father said to him, "James, you have made my child quite a companionable little being!"

My father often left me alone with my uncle; sometimes to write his sermons; sometimes to visit the sick, or give counsel to his poor neighbours; then my uncle used to hold long conversations with me, telling me how I should strive to make my father happy, and endeavour to improve myself when he was gone. Now I began justly to understand why he had taken such pains to keep my father from visiting my mother's grave,—that grave which I often stole privately to look at; but now never without awe and reverence, for my uncle used to tell me what an excellent lady my mother was; and I now thought of her as having been a real mamma, which before seemed an ideal something, no way connected with life. And he told me that the ladies from the Manor-house, who sat in the best pew in the church, were not so graceful, and the best women in

the village were not so good, as was my sweet
mamma; and that if she had lived, I should not have
been forced to pick up a little knowledge from him,
a rough sailor, or to learn to knit and sew of Susan,
but that she would have taught me all ladylike fine
works, and delicate behaviour, and perfect manners,
and would have selected for me proper books, such
as were most fit to instruct my mind, and of which
he nothing knew. If ever in my life I shall have
any proper sense of what is excellent or becoming
in the womanly character, I owe it to these lessons of
my rough unpolished uncle; for, in telling me what
my mother would have made me, he taught me what
to wish to be; and when, soon after my uncle left us,
I was introduced to the ladies at the Manor-house,
instead of hanging down my head with shame, as I
should have done before my uncle came, like a little
village rustic, I tried to speak distinctly, with ease
and a modest gentleness, as my uncle had said my
mother used to do; instead of hanging down my
head abashed, I looked upon them, and thought what
a pretty sight a fine lady was, and how well my
mother must have appeared, since she was so much
more graceful than these high ladies were; and when
I heard them compliment my father on the admirable
behaviour of his child, and say how well he had
brought me up, I thought to myself, "Papa does not
much mind my manners, if I am but a good girl;
but it was my uncle that taught me to behave like

mamma." I cannot now think my uncle was so rough and unpolished as he said he was, for his lessons were so good and so impressive that I shall never forget them, and I hope they will be of use to me as long as I live. He would explain to me the meaning of all the words he used, such as grace and elegance, modest diffidence and affectation, pointing out instances of what he meant by those words, in the manners of the ladies and their young daughters who came to our church; for, besides the ladies of the Manor-house, many of the neighbouring families came to our church, because my father preached so well.

It must have been early in the spring when my uncle went away, for the crocuses were just blown in the garden, and the primroses had begun to peep from under the young budding hedgerows. I cried as if my heart would break, when I had the last sight of him through a little opening among the trees as he went down the road. My father accompanied him to the market-town, from whence he was to proceed in the stage-coach to London. How tedious I thought all Susan's endeavours to comfort me were. The stile where I first saw my uncle came into my mind, and I thought I would go and sit there, and think about that day; but I was no sooner seated there, than I remembered how I had frightened him by taking him so foolishly to my mother's grave, and then again how naughty I had been when I sat muttering to myself at this same stile, wishing that he who had gone so far to buy me books might never come back any more; all my little quarrels with my uncle came into my mind now that I could never play with him again, and it almost broke my heart. I was forced to run into the house to Susan for that consolation I had just before despised.

Some days after this, as I was sitting by the fire with my father, after it was dark, and before the candles were lighted, I gave him an account of my troubled conscience at the church-stile, when I remembered how unkind I had been to my uncle when he first came, and how sorry I still was whenever I thought of the many quarrels I had had with him.

My father smiled, and took hold of my hand, saying, "I will tell you all about this, my little penitent. This is the sort of way in which we all feel when those we love are taken from us. When our dear friends are with us, we go on enjoying their society, without much thought or consideration of the blessing we are possessed of, nor do we too nicely weigh the measure of our daily actions—we let them freely share our kind or our discontented moods; and, if any little bickerings disturb our friendship, it does but the more endear us to each other when we are in a happier temper. But these things come over us like grievous faults when the object of our affection is gone for ever. Your dear mamma and I had no quarrels; yet in the first days of my lonely sorrow how many things came into my mind that I might have done to have made her happier. It is so with you, my child. You did all a child could do to please your uncle, and dearly did he love you; and these little things which now disturb your tender mind, were remembered with delight by your uncle; he was telling me in our last walk, just perhaps as you were thinking about it with sorrow, of the difficulty he had in getting into your good graces when he first came; he will think of these things with pleasure when he is far away. Put away from you this unfounded grief; only let it be a lesson to you to be as kind as possible to those you love; and remember, when they are gone from you, you will never think you had been kind enough. Such feelings as you have now described are the lot of humanity. So you will feel when I am no more, and so will your children feel when you are dead. But your uncle will come back again, Betsy, and we will now think of where we are to get the cage to keep the talking parrot in, he is to bring home; and go and tell Susan to bring the candles, and ask her if the nice cake is almost baked that she promised to give us for our tea."

At this point, my dear Miss Villiers, you thought fit to break off your story, and the wet eyes of your young auditors seemed to confess that you had succeeded in moving their feelings with your pretty narrative. It now fell by lot to the turn of Miss Manners to relate her story, and we were all sufficiently curious to know what so very young an historian had to tell of herself. I shall continue the narratives for the future in the order in which they followed, without mentioning any of the interruptions which occurred from the asking of questions, or from any other cause, unless materially connected with the stories. I shall also leave out the apologies with which you severally thought fit to preface your stories of yourselves, though they were very seasonable in their place, and proceeded from a proper diffidence, because I must not swell my work to too large a size.

Louisa Manners

THE FARMHOUSE

My name is Louisa Manners; I was seven years of age last birthday, which was on the first of May. I remember only four birthdays. The day I was four years old was the first that I recollect. On the morning of that day, as soon as I awoke, I crept into mamma's bed, and said, "Open your eyes, mamma, for it is my birthday. Open your eyes and look at me!" Then mamma told me I should ride in a post-chaise, and see my grandmamma and my sister Sarah. Grandmamma lived at a farmhouse in the country, and I had never in all my life been out of London; no, nor had I ever seen a bit of green grass, except in the Drapers' Garden, which is near my papa's house in Broad Street; nor had I ever rode in a carriage before that happy birthday.

I ran about the house talking of where I was going, and rejoicing so that it was my birthday, that when I got into the chaise I was tired, and fell asleep.

When I awoke, I saw the green fields on both sides of the chaise, and the fields were full, quite full, of bright shining yellow flowers, and sheep and young lambs were feeding in them. I jumped and clapped my hands together for joy, and I cried out, "This is

" 'Abroad in the meadows to see the young lambs,' "

for I knew many of Watts's hymns by heart.

The trees and hedges seemed to fly swiftly by us, and one field, and the sheep, and the young lambs, passed away; and then another field came, and that was full of cows; and then another field, and all the pretty sheep returned; and there was no end of these charming sights till we came quite to grandmamma's house, which stood all alone by itself, no house to be seen at all near it.

Grandmamma was very glad to see me, and she was very sorry that I did not remember her, though I had been so fond of her when she was in town but a few months before. I was quite ashamed of my bad memory. My sister Sarah showed me all the beautiful places about grandmamma's house. She first took me into the farmyard, and I peeped into the barn; there I saw a man thrashing, and as he beat the corn with his flail, he made such a dreadful noise that I was frightened, and ran away; my sister persuaded me to return; she said Will Tasker was very good-natured; then I went back, and peeped at him again; but as I could not reconcile myself to the sound of his flail, or the sight of his black beard, we proceeded to see the rest of the farmyard.

There was no end to the curiosities that Sarah had to show me. There was the pond where the ducks were swimming, and the little wooden houses where the hens slept at night. The hens were feeding all over the yard, and the prettiest little chickens, they were feeding too, and little yellow ducklings that had a hen for their mamma. She was so frightened if they went near the water! Grandmamma says a hen is not esteemed a very wise bird.

We went out of the farmyard into the orchard. Oh, what a sweet place grandmamma's orchard is! There were pear-trees, and apple-trees, and cherry-trees, all in blossom. These blossoms were the prettiest flowers that ever were seen; and among the grass under the trees there grew buttercups, and cowslips, and daffodils, and blue-bells. Sarah told me all their names, and she said I might pick as many of them as ever I pleased.

I filled my lap with flowers, I filled my bosom with flowers, and I carried as many flowers as I could in both my hands; but as I was going into the parlour to show them to my mamma, I stumbled over a threshold which was placed across the parlour, and down I fell with all my treasure.

Nothing could have so well pacified me for the misfortune of my fallen flowers as the sight of a delicious syllabub which happened at that moment to be brought in. Grandmamma said it was a present from the red cow to me because it was my birthday; and then, because it was the first of May, she ordered the syllabub to be placed under the Maybush that grew before the parlour-door, and when we were seated on the grass round it, she helped me the very first to a large glass full of the syllabub, and wished me many happy returns of that day, and then she said I was myself the sweetest little May-blossom in the orchard.

After the syllabub, there was the garden to see, and a most beautiful garden it was;—long and narrow, a straight gravel walk down the middle of it; at the end of the gravel walk there was a green arbour with a bench under it.

There were rows of cabbages and radishes, and peas and beans. I was delighted to see them, for I never saw so much as a cabbage growing out of the ground before.

On one side of this charming garden there were a great many beehives, and the bees sung so prettily.

Mamma said, "Have you nothing to say to these pretty bees, Louisa?" Then I said to them—

"How doth the little busy bee improve each shining hour,
And gather honey all the day from every opening flower."

They had a most beautiful flower-bed to gather it from, quite close under the hives.

I was going to catch one bee, till Sarah told me about their stings, which made me afraid for a long time to go too near their hives; but I went a little nearer, and a little nearer every day, and before I came away from grandmamma's, I grew so bold, I let Will Tasker hold me over the glass windows at the top of the hives, to see them make honey in their own home.

After seeing the garden, I saw the cows milked, and that was the last sight I saw that day; for while I was telling mamma about the cows, I fell fast asleep, and I suppose I was then put to bed.

The next morning my papa and mamma were gone. I cried sadly, but was a little comforted at hearing they would return in a month or two, and fetch me home. I was a foolish little thing then, and did not know how long a month was. Grandmamma gave me a little basket to gather my flowers in. I went into the orchard, and before I had half-filled my basket I forgot all my troubles.

The time I passed at my grandmamma's is always in my mind. Sometimes I think of the good-natured pied cow that would let me stroke her while the dairy-maid was milking her. Then I fancy myself running after the dairy-maid into the nice clean dairy, and see the pans full of milk and cream. Then I remember the wood-house; it had once been a large barn, but being grown old, the wood was kept there. My sister and I used to peep about among the faggots, to find the eggs the hens sometimes left there. Birds' nests we might not look for. Grandmamma was very angry once, when Will Tasker brought home a bird's nest full of pretty speckled eggs for me. She sent him back to the hedge with it again. She said the little birds would not sing any more if their eggs were taken away from them.

A hen, she said, was a hospitable bird, and always laid more eggs than she wanted, on purpose to give her mistress to make puddings and custards with.

I do not know which pleased grandmamma best, when we carried her home a lapful of eggs, or a few violets; for she was particularly fond of violets.

Violets were very scarce; we used to search very carefully for them every morning round by the orchard hedge, and Sarah used to carry a stick in her hand to beat away the nettles; for very frequently the hens left their eggs among the nettles. If we could find eggs and violets too, what happy children we were!

Every day I used to fill my basket with flowers, and for a long time I liked one pretty flower as well as another pretty flower; but Sarah was much wiser than me, and she taught me which to prefer.

Grandmamma's violets were certainly best of all, but they never went in the basket, being carried home, almost flower by flower, as soon as they were found, therefore blue-bells might be said to be the best, for the cowslips were all withered and gone before I learned the true value of flowers. The best blue-bells were those tinged with red; some were so very red that we called them red blue-bells, and these Sarah prized very highly indeed. Daffodils were so plentiful, they were not thought worth gathering unless they were double ones; and buttercups I found were very poor flowers indeed, yet I would pick one now and then, because I knew they were the very same flowers that had delighted me so in the journey; for my papa had told me they were.

I was very careful to love best the flowers which Sarah praised most, yet sometimes, I confess, I have even picked a daisy, though I knew it was the very worst flower of all, because it reminded me of London, and the Drapers' Garden; for, happy as I was at grandmamma's, I could not help sometimes thinking of my papa and mamma, and then I used to tell my sister all about London; how the houses stood all close to each other; what a pretty noise the coaches made; and what a great many people there were in the streets. After we had been talking on these subjects, we generally used to go into the old woodhouse and play at being in London. We used to set up bits of wood for houses; our two dolls we called papa and mamma; in one corner we made a little garden with grass and daisies, and that was to be the Drapers' Garden. I would not have any other flowers here than daisies, because no other grew among the grass in the real Drapers' Garden. Before the time of haymaking came, it was very much talked of. Sarah told me what a merry time it would be, for she remembered everything which had happened for a year or more. She told me how nicely we should throw the hay about. I was very desirous, indeed, to see the hay made.

To be sure, nothing could be more pleasant than the day the orchard was mowed: the hay smelled so sweet, and we might toss it about as much as ever we pleased; but, dear me, we often wish for things that do not prove so happy as we expected; the hay, which was at first so green and smelled so sweet, became yellow and dry, and was carried away in a cart to feed the horses; and then, when it was all gone, and there was no more to play with, I looked upon the naked ground, and perceived what we had lost in these few merry days. Ladies, would you believe it, every flower, blue-bells, daffodils, butter-cups, daisies, all were cut off by the cruel scythe of the mower. No flower was to be seen at all, except here and there a short solitary daisy, that a week before one would not have looked at.

It was a grief, indeed, to me, to lose all my pretty flowers; yet when we are in great distress, there is always, I think, something which happens to comfort us; and so it happened now that gooseberries and currants were almost ripe, which was certainly a very pleasant prospect. Some of them began to turn red, and as we never disobeyed grandmamma we used often to consult together, if it was likely she would permit us to eat them yet; then we would pick a few that looked the ripest, and run to ask her if she thought they were ripe enough to eat, and the uncertainty what her opinion would be made them doubly sweet if she gave us leave to eat them.

When the currants and gooseberries were quite ripe, grandmamma had a sheep-shearing. All the sheep stood under the trees to be sheared. They were brought out of the field by old Spot, the shepherd. I stood at the orchard-gate and saw him drive them all in. When they had cropped off all their wool, they looked very clean, and white, and pretty, but, poor things, they ran shivering about with cold, so that it was a pity to see them. Great preparations were making all day for the sheep-shearing supper. Sarah said a sheep-shearing was not to be compared to a harvest-home, *that* was so much better, for that then the oven was quite full of plum-pudding, and the kitchen was very hot indeed with roasting beef; yet I can assure you there was no want at all of either roast-beef or plum-pudding at the sheep-shearing.

My sister and I were permitted to sit up till it was almost dark, to see the company at supper. They sat at a long oak table, which was finely carved, and as bright as a looking-glass.

I obtained a great deal of praise that day, because I replied so prettily when I was spoken to. My sister was more shy than me; never having lived in London was the reason of that. After the happiest day bedtime will come! We sat up late; but at last grandmamma sent us to bed; yet though we went to bed, we heard many charming songs sung; to be sure, we could not distinguish the words, which was a pity, but the sound of their voices was very loud, and very fine indeed.

The common supper that we had every night was very cheerful. Just before the men came out of the field, a large faggot was flung on the fire; the wood used to crackle and blaze, and smell delightfully; and then the crickets, for they loved the fire, they used to sing; and old Spot, the shepherd, who loved the fire as well as the crickets did, he used to take his place in the chimney corner; after the hottest day in summer, there old Spot used to sit. It was a seat within the fireplace, quite under the chimney, and over his head the bacon hung.

When old Spot was seated, the milk was hung in a skillet over the fire, and then the men used to come and sit down at the long white table.

Pardon me, my dear Louisa, that I interrupted you here. You are a little woman now to what you were then; and I may say to you, that though I loved to hear you prattle of your early recollections, I thought I perceived some ladies present were rather weary of hearing so much of the visit to grandmamma. You may remember I asked you some questions concerning your papa and mamma, which led you to speak of your journey home; but your little town-bred head was so full of the pleasures of a country life, that you first made many apologies that you were unable to tell what happened during the harvest, as unfortunately you were fetched home the very day before it began.

Ann Withers

THE CHANGELING

MY name you know is Withers, but as I once thought I was the daughter of Sir Edward and Lady Harriot Lesley, I shall speak of myself as Miss Lesley, and call Sir Edward and Lady Harriot my father and mother during the period I supposed them entitled to those beloved names. When I was a little girl, it was the perpetual subject of my contemplation that I was an heiress, and the daughter of a baronet; that my mother was the Honourable Lady Harriot; that we had a nobler mansion, infinitely finer pleasure grounds, and equipages more splendid than any of the neighbouring families. Indeed, my good friends, having observed nothing of this error of mine in either of the lives which have hitherto been related, I am ashamed to confess what a proud child I once was. How it happened I cannot tell, for my father was esteemed the best bred man in the country, and the condescension and affability of my mother were universally spoken of.

"Oh, my dear friend," said Miss ——, "it was very natural indeed, if you supposed you possessed these advantages. We make no comparative figure in the county, and my father was originally a man of no consideration at all; and yet I can assure you, both he and mamma had a prodigious deal of trouble to break me off this infirmity when I was very young."—"And do reflect for a moment," said Miss Villiers, "from whence could proceed any pride in me—a poor curate's daughter;—at least any pride worth speaking of; for the difficulty my father had to make me feel myself on an equality with a miller's little daughter who visited me, did not seem an anecdote worth relating. My father, from his profession, is accustomed to look into these things, and whenever he has observed any tendency to this fault in me, and has made me sensible of my error, I, who am rather a weak-spirited girl, have been so much distressed at his reproofs, that to restore me to my own good opinion he would make me sensible that pride is a defect inseparable from human nature; showing me, in our visits to the poorest labourers, how pride would, as he expressed it, 'prettily peep out from under their ragged garbs.' My father dearly loved the poor. In persons of a rank superior to our own humble one, I wanted not much assistance from my father's nice discernment to know that it existed there; and for these latter he would always claim that toleration from me, which he said he observed I was less willing to allow than to the former instances. 'We are told in Holy Writ,' he would say, 'that it is easier for a camel to go through the eye of a needle,

36

than for a rich man to enter into the kingdom of heaven. Surely this is not meant alone to warn the affluent; it must also be understood as an expressive illustration, to instruct the lowly-fortuned man, that he should bear with those imperfections, inseparable from that dangerous prosperity from which he is happily exempt.' But we sadly interrupt your story."

"You are very kind, ladies, to speak with so much indulgence of my foible," said Miss Withers, and was going to proceed, when little Louisa Manners asked, "Pray, are not equipages carriages?"—"Yes, Miss Manners, an equipage is a carriage,"—"Then I am sure if my papa had but one equipage I should be very proud; for once when my papa talked of keeping a one-horse chaise, I never was so proud of anything in my life; I used to dream of riding in it, and imagine I saw my playfellows walking past me in the streets."

"Oh, my dear Miss Manners," replied Miss Withers, "Your young head might well run on a thing so new to you; but you have preached a useful lesson to me in your own pretty rambling story, which I shall not easily forget. When you were speaking with such delight of the pleasure the sight of a farmyard, an orchard, and a narrow slip of kitchen-garden gave you, and could for years preserve so lively the memory of one short ride, and that probably through a flat uninteresting country, I remembered how early I learned to disregard the face of Nature, unless she were decked in picturesque scenery; how wearisome our parks and grounds became to me, unless some improvement were going forward which I thought would attract notice; but those days are gone!"—I will now proceed in my story, and bring you acquainted with my real parents.

Alas! I am a changeling, substituted by my mother for the heiress of the Lesley family; it was for my sake she did this naughty deed; yet, since the truth has been known, it seems to me as if I had been the only sufferer by it; remembering no time when I was not Harriot Lesley, it seems as if the change had taken from me my birthright.

Lady Harriot had intended to nurse her child herself; but being seized with a violent fever soon after its birth, she was not only unable to nurse it, but even to see it for several weeks. I was not quite a month old at this time, when my mother was hired to be Mrs. Lesley's nurse—she had once been a servant in the family—her husband was then at sea.

She had been nursing Miss Lesley a few days, when a girl who had the care of me brought me into the nursery to see my mother. It happened that she wanted something from her own home, which she despatched the girl to fetch, and desired her to leave me till her return. In her absence she changed our clothes; then keeping me to personate the child she was nursing, she sent away the daughter of Sir

Edward to be brought up in her own poor cottage.

When my mother sent away the girl, she affirmed she had not the least intention of committing this bad action; but after she was left alone with us, she looked on me, and then on the little lady-babe, and she wept over me, to think she was obliged to leave me to the charge of a careless girl, debarred from my own natural food, while she was nursing another person's child.

The laced cap and the fine cambric robe of the little Harriot were lying on the table ready to be put on: in these she dressed me, only just to see how pretty her own dear baby would look in missy's fine clothes. When she saw me thus adorned, she said to me, "Oh, my dear Ann, you look as like Missy as anything can be. I am sure my lady herself, if she were well enough to see you, would not know the difference." She said these words aloud, and while she was speaking, a wicked thought came into her head—how easy it would be to change these children! On which she hastily dressed Harriot in my coarse raiment. She had no sooner finished the transformation of Miss Lesley into the poor Ann Withers, than the girl returned and carried her away, without the least suspicion that it was not the same infant that she had brought thither.

It was wonderful that no one discovered that I was not the same child. Every fresh face that came into the room filled the nurse with terror. The servants still continued to pay their compliments to the baby in the same form as usual, saying, how like it is to its papa! Nor did Sir Edward himself perceive the difference, his lady's illness probably engrossing all his attention at the time; though, indeed, gentlemen seldom take much notice of very young children.

When Lady Harriot began to recover, and the nurse saw me in her arms caressed as her own child, all fears of detection were over; but the pangs of remorse then seized her; as the dear sick lady hung with tears of fondness over me, she thought she should have died with sorrow for having so cruelly deceived her.

When I was a year old Mrs. Withers was discharged; and because she had been observed to nurse me with uncommon care and affection, and was seen to shed many tears at parting from me, to reward her fidelity, Sir Edward settled a small pension on her, and she was allowed to come every Sunday to dine in the house-keeper's room, and see her little lady.

When she went home, it might have been expected she would have neglected the child she had so wickedly stolen; instead of which she nursed it with the greatest tenderness, being very sorry for what she had done; all the ease she could ever find for her troubled conscience, was in her extreme care of this injured child; and in the weekly visits to its father's house she constantly brought it with her. At the time I have the earliest recollection of her, she was become a widow, and with the pension Sir Edward allowed her, and some plain work she did for our family, she maintained herself and her supposed daughter. The doting fondness she showed for her child was much talked of; it was said she waited upon it more like a servant than a mother; and it was observed its clothes were always made, as far as her slender means would permit, in the same fashion, and her hair cut and curled in the same form as mine. To this person, as having been my faithful nurse, and to her child, I was always taught to show particular civility, and the little girl was always brought into the nursery to play with me. Ann was a little delicate thing, and remarkably well-behaved; for though so much indulged in every other respect, my mother was very attentive to her manners.

As the child grew older, my mother became very uneasy about her education. She was so very desirous of having her well-behaved, that she feared to send her to school, lest she should learn ill manners among the village children, with whom she never suffered her to play; and she was such a poor scholar herself, that she could teach her little or nothing. I heard her relate this her distress to my own maid, with tears in her eyes, and I formed a resolution to beg of my parents that I might have Ann for a companion, and that she might be allowed to take lessons with me of my governess.

My birthday was then approaching, and on that

day I was always indulged in the privilege of asking some peculiar favour.

"And what boon has my annual petitioner to beg today?" said my father, as he entered the breakfast-room on the morning of my birthday. Then I told him of the great anxiety expressed by Nurse Withers concerning her daughter; how much she wished it was in her power to give her an education that would enable her to get her living without hard labour. I set the good qualities of Ann Withers in the best light I could, and in conclusion, I begged she might be permitted to partake with me in education, and become my companion. "This is a very serious request indeed, Harriot," said Sir Edward; "your mother and I must consult together on the subject." The result of this conversation was favourable to my wishes; in a few weeks my foster-sister was taken into the house, and placed under the tuition of my governess.

To me, who had hitherto lived without any companions of my own age except occasional visitors, the idea of a playfellow constantly to associate with was very pleasant; and after the first shyness of feeling her altered situation was over, Ann seemed as much at her ease as if she had always been brought up in our house. I became very fond of her, and took pleasure in showing her all manner of attentions; which so far won on her affections, that she told me she had a secret intrusted to her by her mother, which she had promised never to reveal as long as her mother lived, but that she almost wished to confide it to me, because I was such a kind friend to her; yet, having promised never to tell it till the death of her mother, she was afraid to tell it to me. At first I assured her that I would never press her to the disclosure, for that promises of secrecy were to be held sacred; but whenever we fell into any confidential kind of conversation, this secret seemed always ready to come out. Whether she or I were most to blame, I know not, though I own I could not help giving frequent hints how well I could keep a secret. At length she told me what I have before related, namely, that she was in truth the daughter of Sir Edward and Lady Lesley, and I the child of her supposed mother.

When I was first in possession of this wonderful secret, my heart burned to reveal it. I thought how praiseworthy it would be in me to restore to my friend the rights of her birth; yet I thought only of becoming her patroness, and raising her to her proper rank; it never occurred to me that my own degradation must necessarily follow. I endeavoured to persuade her to let me tell this important affair to my parents: this she positively refused. I expressed wonder that she should so faithfully keep this secret for an unworthy woman, who in her infancy had done her such an injury.

"Oh!" said she, "you do not know how much she loves me, or you would not wonder that I never resent that. I have seen her grieve and be so very sorry on my account, that I would not bring her into more trouble for any good that could happen to myself. She has often told me, that since the day she changed us, she has never known what it is to have a happy moment; and when she returned home from nursing you, finding me very thin and sickly, how her heart smote her for what she had done; and then she nursed and fed me with such anxious care, that she grew much fonder of me than if I had been her own; and that on the Sundays, when she used to bring me here, it was more pleasure to her to see me in my own father's house, than it was to her to see you, her real child. The shyness you showed towards her while you were very young, and the forced civility you seemed to affect as you grew older, always appeared like ingratitude towards her who had done so much for you. My mother has desired me to disclose this after her death, but I do not believe I shall ever mention it then, for I should be sorry to bring any reproach even on her memory."

In a short time after this important discovery, Ann was sent home to pass a few weeks with her mother, on the occasion of the unexpected arrival of some visitors to our house; they were to bring children with them, and these I was to consider as my own guests.

In the expected arrival of my young visitants, and in making preparations to entertain them, I had little leisure to deliberate on what conduct I should pursue with regard to my friend's secret. Something must be done, I thought, to make her amends for the injury she had sustained, and I resolved to consider the matter attentively on her return. Still my mind ran on conferring favours. I never considered myself as transformed into the dependent person. Indeed, Sir Edward at this time set me about a task which occupied the whole of my attention; he proposed that I should write a little interlude, after the manner of the French *Petites Pieces;* and to try my ingenuity, no one was to see it before the representation, except the performers, myself, and my little friends, who, as they were all younger than me, could not be expected to lend me much assistance. I have already told you what a proud girl I was. During the writing of this piece, the receiving of my young friends, and the instructing them in their several parts, I never felt myself of so much importance. With Ann, my pride had somewhat slumbered; the difference of our rank left no room for competition; all was complacency and good-humour on my part, and affectionate gratitude, tempered with respect, on hers. But here I had full room to show courtesy, to affect those graces, to imitate that elegance of manners practised by Lady Harriot to their mothers. I was to be their instructress in action and in attitudes, and to receive their praises and their admiration of my theatrical genius. It was a new scene of triumph for me, and I might then be said to be in the very height of my glory.

If the plot of my piece, for the invention of which they so highly praised me, had been indeed my own, all would have been well; but unhappily I borrowed from a source which made my drama end far differently from what I intended it should. In the catastrophe I lost not only the name I personated in the piece, but with it my own name also; and all my rank and consequence in the world fled from me for ever. My father presented me with a beautiful writing-desk for the use of my new authorship; my silver standish was placed upon it; a quire of gilt paper was before me. I took out a parcel of my best crow quills, and down I sat in the greatest form imaginable.

I conjecture I have no talent for invention; certain it is, that when I sat down to compose my piece, no story would come into my head, but the story which Ann had so lately related to me. Many sheets were scrawled over in vain, I could think of nothing else; still the babies and the nurse were before me in all the *minutiæ* of description Ann had given them. The costly attire of the lady-babe—the homely garb of the cottage-infant—the affecting address of the fond mother to her own offspring—then the charming *équivoque* in the change of the children; it all looked so dramatic;—it was a play ready-made to my hands. The invalid mother would form the pathetic, the silly exclamations of the servants the ludicrous, and the nurse was nature itself. It is true, I had a few scruples that it might, should it come to the knowledge of Ann, be construed into something very like a breach of confidence. But she was at home, and might never happen to hear of the subject of my piece and if she did, why, it was only making some handsome apology. To a dependent companion, to whom I had been so very great a friend, it was not necessary to be so very particular about such a triffle.

Thus I reasoned as I wrote my drama, beginning with the title, which I called "The Changeling," and ending with these words : *The curtain drops, while the lady clasps the baby in her arms, and the nurse sighs audibly.* I invented no new incident; I simply wrote the story as Ann had told it to me, in the best blank verse I was able to compose.

By the time it was finished, the company had arrived. The casting the different parts was my next care. The Honourable Augustus M——, a young gentleman of five years of age, undertook to play the father. He was only to come in and say, *How does my little darling do to-day?* The three Miss——s were to be the servants; they too had only single lines to speak.

As these four were all very young performers, we made them rehearse many times over, that they might walk in and out with proper decorum; but the performance was stopped before their entrances and their exits arrived. I complimented Lady

Elizabeth, the sister of Augustus, who was the eldest of the young ladies, with the choice of the lady mother or the nurse. She fixed on the former; she was to recline on a sofa, and, affecting ill health, speak some eight or ten lines, which began with— *O that I could my precious baby see!* To her cousin Miss Emily ——, was given the girl who had the care of the nurse's child; two dolls were to personate the two children; and the principal character of the nurse I had the pleasure to perform myself. It consisted of several speeches, and a very long soliloquy during the changing of the children's clothes.

The elder brother of Augustus, a gentleman of fifteen years of age, who refused to mix in our childish drama, yet condescended to paint the scenes; and our dresses were got up by my own maid.

When we thought ourselves quite perfect in our several parts, we announced it for representation. Sir Edward and Lady Harriot, with their visitors, the parents of my young troop of comedians, honoured us with their presence. The servants were also permitted to go into a music-gallery, which was at the end of a ball-room we had chosen for our theatre.

As author and principal performer, standing before a noble audience, my mind was too much engaged with the arduous task I had undertaken, to glance my eyes towards the music-gallery, or I might have seen two more spectators there than I expected. Nurse Withers and her daughter Ann were there; they had been invited by the housekeeper to be present at the representation of Miss Lesley's play.

In the midst of the performance, as I, in the character of the nurse, was delivering the wrong child to the girl, there was an exclamation from the music-gallery of "Oh! it's all true! it's all true!" This was followed by a bustle among the servants, and screams as of a person in an hysteric fit. Sir Edward came forward to inquire what was the matter. He saw it was Mrs. Withers who had fallen into a fit. Ann was weeping over her, and crying out, "O Miss Lesley, you have told all in the play!"

Mrs. Withers was brought out into the ball-room; there, with tears and in broken accents, with every sign of terror and remorse, she soon made a full confession of her so-long-concealed guilt.

The strangers assembled to see our childish mimicry of passion were witnesses to a highly-wrought dramatic scene in real life. I had intended they should see the curtain drop without any discovery of the deceit; unable to invent any new incident, I left the conclusion imperfect as I found it; but they saw a more strict poetical justice done; they saw the rightful child restored to its parents, and the nurse overwhelmed with shame, and threatened with severest punishment.

"Take this woman," said Sir Edward, "and lock her up, till she be delivered into the hands of justice."

Ann, on her knees, implored mercy for her

mother.   Addressing the children, who were gathered round her, "Dear ladies," said she, "help me, on your knees help me, to beg forgiveness for my mother."   Down the young ones all dropped— even Lady Elizabeth bent on her knee.   "Sir Edward, pity her distress, Sir Edward, pardon her!"   All joined in the petition, except one whose voice ought to have been loudest in the appeal.   No word, no accent came from me.   I hung over Lady Harriot's chair, weeping as if my heart would break; but I wept for my own fallen fortunes, not for my mother's sorrow.

I thought within myself, "If in the integrity of my heart, refusing to participate in this unjust secret, I had boldly ventured to publish the truth, I might have had some consolation in the praises which so generous an action would have merited; but it is through the vanity of being supposed to have written a pretty story that I have meanly broken my faith with my friend, and unintentionally proclaimed the disgrace of my mother and myself."   While thoughts like these were passing through my mind, Ann had obtained my mother's pardon.   Instead of being sent away to confinement and the horrors of a prison, she was given by Sir Edward into the care of the housekeeper, who had orders from Lady Harriot to see her put to bed and properly attended to, for again this wretched woman had fallen into a fit.

Ann would have followed my mother, but Sir

Edward brought her back, telling her that she should see her when she was better. He then led her towards Lady Harriot, desiring her to embrace her child; she did so, and I saw her, as I had phrased it in the play, *clasped in her mother's arms*.

This scene had greatly affected the spirits of Lady Harriot; through the whole of it, it was with difficulty she had been kept from fainting, and she was now led into the drawing-room by the ladies. The gentlemen followed, talking with Sir Edward of the astonishing instance of filial affection they had just seen in the earnest pleadings of the child for her supposed mother.

Ann, too, went with them, and was conducted by her whom I had always considered as my own particular friend. Lady Elizabeth took hold of her hand and said, "Miss Lesley, will you permit me to conduct you to the drawing-room?"

I was left weeping behind the chair where Lady Harriot had sat, and, as I thought, quite alone. A something had before twitched my frock two or three times so slightly I had scarcely noticed it; a little head now peeped round, and looking up in my face, said, "She is not Miss Lesley!" It was the young Augustus; he had been sitting at my feet, but I had not observed him. He then started up, and taking hold of my hand with one of his, with the other holding fast by my clothes, he led, or rather dragged me, into the midst of the company assembled in the drawing-room. The vehemence of his manner, his little face as red as fire, caught every eye. The ladies smiled, and one gentleman laughed in a most unfeeling manner. His elder brother patted him on the head, and said, "Your are a humane little fellow: Elizabeth, we might have thought of this."

Very kind words were now spoken to me by Sir Edward, and he called me Harriot, precious name now grown to me. Lady Harriot kissed me, and said she would never forget how long she had loved me as her child. These were comfortable words; but I heard echoed round the room, "Poor thing, *she* cannot help it—I am sure *she* is to be pitied. Dear Lady Harriot, how kind, how considerate you are!" Ah! what a deep sense of my altered condition did I then feel!

"Let the young ladies divert themselves in another room," said Sir Edward; "and, Harriot, take your new sister with you, and help her to entertain your friends." Yes, he called me Harriot again, and afterwards invented new names for his daughter and me, and always called us by them, apparently in jest; yet I knew it was only because he would not hurt me with hearing our names reversed. When Sir Edward desired us to show the children into another room, Ann and I walked towards the door. A new sense of humiliation arose—how could I go out at the door before Miss Lesley?—I stood irresolute; she drew back. The elder brother of my friend Augustus assisted me in this perplexity; pushing us all forward, as if in a playful mood, he drove us indiscriminately before him, saying, "I will make one among you to-day." He had never joined in our sports before.

My luckless play, that sad instance of my duplicity, was never once mentioned to me afterwards, not even by any one of the children who had acted in it; and I must also tell you how considerate an old lady was at the time about our dresses. As soon as she perceived things growing very serious, she hastily stripped off the upper garments we wore to represent our different characters. I think I should have died with shame if the child had led me into the drawing-room in the mummery I had worn to represent a nurse. This good lady was of another essential service to me; for perceiving an irresolution in every one how they should behave to us, which distressed me very much, she contrived to place Miss Lesley above me at table, and called her Miss Lesley, and me Miss Withers; saying at the same time in a low voice, but as if she meant I should hear her, "It is better these things should be done at once, then they are over." My heart thanked her, for I felt the truth of what she said.

My poor mother continued very ill for many weeks; no medicine could remove the extreme dejection of spirits she laboured under. Sir Edward sent for the clergyman of the parish to give her religious consolation. Every day he came to visit her, and he would always take Miss Lesley and me into the room with him. I think, Miss Villiers, your father must be just such another man as Dr. Wheelding, our worthy rector; just so I think he would have soothed the troubled conscience of my repentant mother. How feelingly, how kindly he used to talk of mercy and forgiveness!

My heart was softened by my own misfortunes and the sight of my penitent suffering mother. I felt that she was now my only parent; I strove, earnestly strove to love her; yet ever when I looked in her face, she would seem to me to be the very identical person whom I should have once thought sufficiently honoured by a slight inclination of the head, and a civil "How do you do, Mrs. Withers?" One day, as Miss Lesley was hanging over her with her accustomed fondness, Dr. Wheelding reading in a prayerbook, and, as I thought, not at that moment regarding us, I threw myself on my knees and silently prayed that I too might be able to love my mother.

Dr. Wheelding had been observing me; he took me into the garden, and drew from me the subject of my petition.

"Your prayers, my good young lady," said he, "I hope are heard; sure I am they have caused me to adopt a resolution which, as it will enable you to see your mother frequently, will, I hope, greatly assist your pious wishes. I will take your mother home with me to superintend my family. Under my roof, doubtless, Sir Edward will often permit you to see her. Perform your duty towards her as well as you possibly can. Affection is the growth of time. With such good wishes in your young heart, do not despair that in due time it will assuredly spring up."

With the approbation of Sir Edward and Lady Harriot, my mother was removed in a few days to Dr. Wheelding's house. There she soon recovered; there she at present resides. She tells me she loves me almost as well as she did when I was a baby, and we both wept at parting when I came to school.

Here, perhaps, I ought to conclude my story, which I fear has been a tedious one; permit me, however, to say a few words concerning the time which elapsed since the discovery of my birth until my arrival here.

It was on the fifth day of —— that I was known to be Ann Withers, and the daughter of my supposed nurse. The company who were witness to my disgrace departed in a few days, and I felt relieved from some part of the mortification I hourly experienced. For every fresh instance even of kindness or attention I experienced went to my heart, that I should be forced to feel thankful for it.

Circumstanced as I was, surely I had nothing justly to complain of. The conduct of Sir Edward and Lady Harriot was kind in the extreme; still preserving every appearance of a parental tenderness for me, but ah! I might no longer call them by the dear names of father and mother. Formerly, when speaking of them, I used, proud of their titles, to delight to say, "Sir Edward or Lady Harriot did this, or this;" now I would give worlds to say, "My father or my mother."

I should be perfectly unkind if I were to complain of Miss Lesley—indeed, I have not the least cause of complaint against her. As my companion, her affection and her gratitude had been unbounded; and now that it was my turn to be the humble friend, she tried by every means in her power to make me think she felt the same respectful gratitude which in her dependent station she had so naturally displayed.

Only in a few rarely constituted minds does that true attentive kindness spring up, that delicacy of feeling, which enters into every trivial thing is ever awake and keeping watch lest it should offend. Myself, though educated with the extremest care, possessed but little of this virtue. Virtue I call it, though among men it is termed politeness; for since the days of my humiliating reverse of fortune I have learned its value.

I feel quite ashamed to give instances of any deficiency I observed, or thought I have observed, in Miss Lesley. Now I am away from her, and dispassionately speaking of it, it seems as if my own soreness of temper had made me fancy things. I really believe now that I was mistaken; but Miss Lesley had been so highly praised for her filial tenderness, I thought at last she seemed to make a parade about it, and used to run up to my mother, and affect to be more glad to see her than she really was after a time; and I think Dr. Wheelding thought so by a little hint he once dropped. But he, too, might be mistaken, for he was very partial to me.

I am under the greatest obligation in the world to this good Dr. Wheelding. He has made my mother quite a respectable woman, and I am sure it is owing a great deal to him that she loves me so well as she does.

And here, though it may seem a little out of place, let me stop to assure you, that if I could ever have had any doubt of the sincerity of Miss Lesley's affection towards me, her behaviour on the occasion of my coming here ought completely to efface it. She entreated with many tears, and almost the same energy with which she pleaded for forgiveness for my mother, that I might not be sent away. But she was not alike successful in her supplications.

Miss Lesley had made some progress in reading and writing during the time she was my companion only; it was highly necessary that every exertion should be now made—the whole house was, as I may say, in requisition for her instruction; Sir Edward and Lady Harriot devoted great part of the day to this purpose. A well-educated young person was taken under our governess to assist her in her labours, and to teach Miss Lesley music. A drawing-master was engaged to reside in the house.

At this time I was not remarkably forward in my education. My governess being a native of France, I spoke French very correctly, and I had made some progress in Italian; but I had had the instruction of masters only during the few months in the year we usually passed in London.

Music I never had the least ear for; I could scarcely be taught my notes. This defect in me was always particularly regretted by my mother, she being an excellent performer herself, both on the piano and on the harp. I think I have some taste for drawing; but as Lady Harriot did not particularly excel in this, I lost so much time in the summer months, practising only under my governess, that I made no great proficiency even in this my favourite art. But Miss Lesley, with all these advantages which I have named, —everybody so eager to instruct her, she so willing to learn—everything so new and delightful to her, how could it happen otherwise? she in a short time became a little prodigy. What best pleased Lady Harriot was, after she had conquered the first difficulties, she discovered a wonderful talent for music. Here she was her mother's own girl indeed—she had the same sweet-toned voice—the same delicate finger. Her musical governess had little now to do; for as soon as Lady Harriot perceived this excellence in her, she gave up all company and devoted her whole time to instructing her daughter in this science.

Nothing makes the heart ache with such a hopeless heavy pain, as envy.

I had felt deeply before, but till now I could not be said to envy Miss Lesley. All day long the notes of the harp or the piano spoke sad sounds to me of the loss of a loved mother's heart.

To have in a manner two mothers, and Miss Lesley to engross them both, was too much indeed.

It was at this time that one day I had been wearied with hearing Lady Harriot play one long piece of Haydn's music after another to her enraptured daughter. We were to walk with our governess to Dr. Wheelding's that morning; and after Lady Harriot had left the room, and we were quite ready for our walk, Miss Lesley would not leave the instrument for I know not how long.

It was on that day that I thought she was not quite honest in her expressions of joy at the sight of my poor mother, who had been waiting at the garden-gate near two hours to see her arrive; yet she might be, for the music had put her in remarkably good spirits that morning.

Oh, the music quite, quite won Lady Harriot's heart! Till Miss Lesley began to play so well, she often lamented the time it would take before her daughter would have the air of a person of fashion's child. It was my part of the general instruction to give her lessons on this head. We used to make a kind of play of it, which we called lectures on fashionable manners: it was a pleasant amusement to me, a sort of keeping up the memory of past times. But now the music was always in the way. The last time it was talked of, Lady Harriot said her daughter's time was too precious to be taken up with such trifling.

I must own that the music had that effect on Miss Lesley, as to render these lectures less necessary, which I will explain to you; but first let me assure you that Lady Harriot was by no means in the habit of saying things of this kind. It was almost a solitary instance; I could give you a thousand instances the very reverse of this, in her as well as in Sir Edward. How kindly, how frequently, would they remind me, that to me alone it was owing that they ever knew their child! calling the day on which I was a petitioner for the admittance of Ann into the house, the blessed birthday of their generous girl.

Neither dancing, nor any foolish lectures, could do much for Miss Lesley; she remained for some time wanting in gracefulness of carriage; but all that is usually attributed to dancing, music finally effected. When she was sitting before the instrument, a resemblance to her mother became apparent to every eye. Her attitudes and the expression of her countenance were the very same. This soon followed her into everything; all was ease and natural grace; for the music, and with it the idea of Lady Harriot, was always in her thoughts. It was a pretty sight to see the daily improvement in her person, even to me, poor envious girl that I was.

Soon after Lady Harriot had hurt me by calling my little efforts to improve her daughter trifling, she made me large amends in a very kind and most unreserved conversation that she held with me.

She told me all the struggles she had had at first to feel a maternal tenderness for her daughter; and she frankly confessed, that she had now gained so much on her affections that she feared she had too much neglected the solemn promise she had made me, *Never to forget how long she had loved me as her child.*

Encouraged by her returning kindness, I owned how much I had suffered; and ventured to express my fears that I had hardly courage enough to bear the sight of my former friends under a new designation, as I must now appear to them on our removal to London, which was expected to take place in a short time.

A few days after this she told me in the gentlest manner possible that Sir Edward and herself were of opinion it would conduce to my happiness to pass a year or two at school.

I knew that this proposal was kindly intended to spare me the mortification I so much dreaded; therefore I endeavoured to submit to my hard fate with cheerfulness, and prepared myself, not without reluctance, to quit a mansion which had been the scene of so many enjoyments, and latterly of such very different feelings.

Elinor Forester

WHEN I was very young, I had the misfortune to lose my mother. My father very soon married again. The morning of the day on which that event took place, my father set me on his knee, and as he often used to do after the death of my mother, he called me his dear little orphaned Elinor; and then he asked me if I loved Miss Saville. I replied "Yes." Then he said, this dear lady was going to be so kind as to be married to him, and that she was to live with us and be my mamma. My father told me this with such pleasure in his looks, that I thought it must be a very fine thing indeed to have a new mamma; and on his saying it was time for me to be dressed against his return from church, I ran in great spirits to tell the good news in the nursery. I found my maid and the housemaid looking out of the window to see my father get into his carriage, which was newly painted; the servants had new liveries and fine white ribands in their hats; and then I perceived my father had left off his mourning. The maids were dressed in new coloured gowns and white ribands. On the table I saw a new muslin frock trimmed with fine lace, ready for me to put on. I skipped about the room quite in an ecstasy.

When the carriage drove from the door, the house-keeper came in to bring the maids new white gloves. I repeated to her the words I had just heard, that that dear lady, Miss Saville, was going to be married to papa, and that she was to live with us and be my mamma.

The housekeeper shook her head, and said, "Poor thing! how soon children forget everything!"

I could not imagine what she meant by my forgetting everything, for I instantly recollected poor mamma used to say I had an excellent memory.

The women began to draw on their white gloves, and the seams rending in several places, Ann said, "This is just the way our gloves served us at my mistress's funeral." The other checked her, and said, "Hush!" I was then thinking of some instances in which my mamma had praised my memory, and this reference to her funeral fixed her idea in my mind.

From the time of her death no one had ever spoken to me of my mamma, and I had apparently forgotten her; yet I had a habit, which perhaps had not been observed, of taking my little stool, which had been my mamma's footstool, and a doll which my mamma had dressed for me while she was sitting in her elbow-chair, her head supported with pillows. With these in my hands, I used to go to the door of the room in which I had seen her in her last illness; and after trying to open it, and peeping through the keyhole, from whence I could just see a glimpse of the crimson curtains, I used to sit down on the stool before the door, and play with my doll, and sometimes sing to it mamma's pretty song of "Balow my babe;" imitating as well as I could the weak voice in which she used to sing it to me. My mamma had a very sweet voice. I remember now the gentle tone in which she used to say my prattle did not disturb her.

When I was dressed in my new frock, I wished poor mamma was alive to see how fine I was on papa's wedding-day, and I ran to my favourite station at her bedroom door. There I sat thinking of my mamma, and trying to remember exactly how she used to look; because I foolishly imagined that Miss Saville was to be changed into something like my own mother, whose pale and delicate appearance in her last illness was all that I retained of her remembrance.

When my father returned home with his bride, he walked upstairs to look for me, and my new mamma followed him. They found me at my mother's door earnestly looking through the keyhole. I was thinking so intently on my mother, that when my father said, "Here is your new mamma, my Elinor," I turned round and began to cry, for no other reason than because she had a very high colour, and I remembered my mamma was very pale; she had bright black eyes, my mother's were mild blue eyes;

and that instead of the wrapping gown and close cap in which I remembered my mamma, she was dressed in all her bridal decorations.

I said, "Miss Saville shall not be my mamma," and I cried till I was sent away in disgrace.

Every time I saw her for several days, the same notion came into my head that she was not a bit more like mamma than when she was Miss Saville. My father was very angry when he saw how shy I continued to look at her; but she always said, "Never mind! Elinor and I shall soon be better friends."

One day, when I was very naughty indeed, for I would not speak one word to either of them, my papa took his hat and walked out, quite in a passion. When he was gone, I looked up at my new mamma, expecting to see her very angry too; but she was smiling and looking very good-naturedly upon me; and she said, "Now we are alone together, my pretty little daughter, let us forget papa is angry with us, and tell me why you were peeping through that door the day your papa brought me home, and you cried so at the sight of me." "Because mamma used to be there," I replied. When she heard me say this, she fell a-crying very sadly indeed; and I was so very sorry to hear her cry so, that I forgot I did not love her, and I went up to her and said, "Don't cry, I won't be naughty any more, I won't peep through the door any more."

Then she said I had a little kind heart, and I should

not have any occasion, for she would take me into the room herself; and she rang the bell, and ordered the key of that room to be brought to her; and the housekeeper brought it, and tried to persuade her not to go. But she said, "I must have my own way in this;" and she carried me in her arms into my mother's room.

Oh, I was so pleased to be taken into mamma's room. I pointed out to her all the things that I remembered to have belonged to mamma, and she encouraged me to tell her all the little incidents which had dwelt on my memory concerning her. She told me that she went to school with mamma when she was a little girl, and that I should come into this room with her every day when papa was gone out, and she would tell me stories of mamma when she was a little girl no bigger than me.

When my father came home we were walking in a garden at the back of our house, and I was showing her mamma's geraniums, and telling her what pretty flowers they had when mamma was alive.

My father was astonished; and he said, "Is this the sullen Elinor? what has worked this miracle?" "Ask no questions," she replied, "or you will disturb our new-born friendship. Elinor has promised to love me, and she says, too, that she will call me 'mamma.'" "Yes, I will,—mamma, mamma, mamma," I replied, and hung about her with the greatest fondness.

After this she used to pass great part of the mornings with me in my mother's room, which was now made the repository of all my playthings, and also my schoolroom. Here my new mamma taught me to read. I was a sad little dunce, and scarcely knew my letters. My own mamma had often said, when she got better she would hear me read every day, but as she never got better, it was not her fault. I now began to learn very fast, for when I said my lesson well, I was always rewarded with some pretty story of my mother's childhood; and these stories generally contained some little hints that were instructive to me, and which I greatly stood in want of; for, between improper indulgence and neglect, I had many faulty ways.

In this kind manner my mother-in-law has instructed and improved me, and I love her because she was my mother's friend when they were young. She has been my only instructress, for I never went to school till I came here. She would have continued to teach me, but she has not time, for she has a little baby of her own now, and that is the reason I came to school.

Margaret Green

THE YOUNG MAHOMETAN

My father has been dead nearly three years. Soon after his death, my mother being left in reduced circumstances, she was induced to accept the offer of Mrs. Beresford, an elderly lady of large fortune, to live in her house as her companion and the superintendent of her family. This lady was my godmother, and as I was my mother's only child, she very kindly permitted her to have me with her.

Mrs. Beresford lived in a large old family mansion; she kept no company, and never moved except from the breakfast-parlour to the eating-room, and from thence to the drawing-room to tea.

Every morning when she first saw me, she used to nod her head very kindly, and say, "How do you do, little Margaret?" But I do not recollect she ever spoke to me during the remainder of the day: except indeed, after I had read the psalms and the chapters, which was my daily task; then she used constantly to observe that I improved in my reading, and frequently added, "I never heard a child read so distinctly."

She had been remarkably fond of needlework, and her conversation with my mother was generally the history of some pieces of work she had formerly done; the dates when they were begun, and when finished; what had retarded their progress, and what had hastened their completion. If occasionally any other events were spoken of, she had no other chronology to reckon by, than in the recollection of what carpet, what sofa-cover, what set of chairs, were in the frame at that time.

I believe my mother is not particularly fond of needlework; for in my father's lifetime I never saw her amuse herself in this way; yet, to oblige her kind patroness, she undertook to finish a large carpet which the old lady had just begun when her eyesight failed her. All day long my mother used to sit at the frame, talking of the shades of the worsted, and the beauty of the colours—Mrs. Beresford seated in a chair near her, and, though her eyes were so dim she could hardly distinguish one colour from another, watching through her spectacles the progress of the work.

When my daily portion of reading was over, I had a taste of needlework, which generally lasted half an hour. I was not allowed to pass more time in reading or work, because my eyes were very weak, for which reason I was always set to read in the large-print family Bible. I was very fond of reading; and when I could, unobserved, steal a few minutes as they were intent on their work, I used to delight to read in the historical part of the Bible; but this, because of my eyes, was a forbidden pleasure; and the Bible never being removed out of the room, it was only for a short time together that I dared softly to lift up the leaves and peep into it.

As I was permitted to walk in the garden, or wander about the house whenever I pleased, I used to leave the parlour for hours together, and make out my own solitary amusement as well as I could. My first visit was always to a very large hall, which, from being paved with marble, was called the marble hall. In this hall, while Mrs. Beresford's husband was living, the tenants used to be feasted at Christmas.

The heads of the twelve Cæsars were hung round the hall. Every day I mounted on the chairs to look at them, and to read the inscriptions underneath, till I became perfectly familiar with their names and features.

Hogarth's prints were below the Cæsars: I was very fond of looking at them, and endeavouring to make out their meaning.

An old broken battledore and some shuttlecocks, with most of the feathers missing, were on a marble slab in one corner of the hall, which constantly reminded me that there had once been younger inhabitants here than the old lady and her gray-headed servants. In another corner stood a marble figure of a satyr; every day I laid my hand on his shoulder to feel how cold he was.

This hall opened into a room full of family portraits. They were all in the dresses of former times: some were old men and women, and some were children. I used to long to have a fairy's power to call the children down from their frames to play with me. One little girl in particular, who hung by the side of a glass door which opened into the garden, I often invited to walk there with me, but she still kept her station—one arm round a little lamb's neck, and in her hand a large bunch of roses. From this room I usually proceeded to the garden.

When I was weary of the garden I wandered over the rest of the house. The best suite of rooms I never saw by any other light than what glimmered through the tops of the window-shutters, which, however, served to show the carved chimney-pieces, and the curious old ornaments about the rooms; but the worked furniture and carpets of which I heard such constant praises I could have but an imperfect sight of, peeping under the covers which were kept over them, by the dim light; for I constantly lifted up a corner of the envious cloth that hid these highly-praised rarities from my view.

The bedrooms were also regularly explored by me, as well to admire the antique furniture, as for the sake of contemplating the tapestry hangings, which were full of Bible history. The subject of the one which chiefly attracted my attention was Hagar and her son Ishmael. Every day I admired the beauty of the youth, and pitied the forlorn state of him and his mother in the wilderness. At the end of the gallery into which these tapestry rooms opened, was one door which, having often in vain attempted to open, I concluded to be locked; and finding myself shut out, I was very desirous of seeing what it contained; and though still foiled in the attempt, I every day endeavoured to turn the lock, which—whether by constantly trying I loosened, being probably a very old one, or that the door was not locked but fastened tight by time, I know not—to my great joy, as I was one day trying the lock as usual, it gave way, and I found myself in this so-long-desired room.

It proved to be a very large library. This was indeed a precious discovery. I looked round on the books with the greatest delight. I thought I would read them every one. I now forsook all my favourite haunts, and passed all my time here. I took down first one book, then another.

If you never spent whole mornings alone in a large library, you cannot conceive the pleasure of taking down books in the constant hope of finding an entertaining book among them; yet, after many days, meeting with nothing but disappointment, it becomes less pleasant. All the books within my reach were folios of the gravest cast. I could understand very little that I read in them, and the old dark print and the length of the lines made my eyes ache.

When I had almost resolved to give up the search as fruitless, I perceived a volume lying in an obscure corner of the room. I opened it. It was a charming print; the letters were almost as large as the type of the family Bible. In the first page I looked into I saw the name of my favourite Ishmael, whose face I knew so well from the tapestry, and whose history I had often read in the Bible.

I sat myself down to read this book with the greatest eagerness. The title of it was *Mahometanism Explained.* It was a very improper book, for it contained a false history of Abraham and his descendants.

I shall be quite ashamed to tell you the strange effect it had on me. I know it was very wrong to read any book without permission to do so. If my time were to come over again, I would go and tell my mamma that there was a library in the house, and ask her to permit me to read a little while every day in some book that she might think proper to select for me. But unfortunately I did not then recollect that I ought to do this; the reason of my strange forgetfulness might be that my mother, following the example of her patroness, had almost wholly discontinued talking to me. I scarcely ever heard a word addressed to me from morning to night. If it were not for the old servants saying, "Good morning to you, Miss Margaret!" as they passed me in the long passages, I should have been the greatest part of the day in as perfect a solitude as Robinson Crusoe. It must have been because I was never spoken to at all

74

that I forgot what was right and what was wrong, for I do not believe that I ever remembered I was doing wrong all the time I was reading in the library. A great many of the leaves in *Mahometanism Explained* were torn out, but enough remained to make me imagine that Ishmael was the true son of Abraham; I read here that the true descendants of Abraham were known by a light which streamed from the middle of their foreheads. It said that Ishmael's father and mother first saw this light streaming from his forehead as he was lying asleep in the cradle. I was very sorry so many of the leaves were torn out, for it was as entertaining as a fairy tale. I used to read the history of Ishmael, and then go and look at him in the tapestry, and then read his history again. When I had almost learned the history of Ishmael by heart, I read the rest of the book, and then I came to the history of Mahomet, who was there said to be the last descendant of Abraham.

If Ishmael had engaged so much of my thoughts, now much more so must Mahomet? His history was full of nothing but wonders from the beginning to the end. The book said that those who believed all the wonderful stories which were related of Mahomet were called Mahometans, and True Believers:—I concluded that I must be a Mahometan, for I believed every word I read.

At length I met with something which I also believed, though I trembled as I read it. This was, that after we are dead we are to pass over a narrow bridge, which crosses a bottomless gulf. The bridge was described to be no wider than a silken thread; and it is said that all who were not Mahometans would slip on one side of this bridge, and drop into the tremendous gulf that had no bottom. I considered myself as a Mahometan, yet I was perfectly giddy whenever I thought of passing over this bridge.

One day, seeing the old lady totter across the room, a sudden terror seized me, for I thought how would she ever be able to get over the bridge? Then too it was that I first recollected that my mother would also be in imminent danger; for I imagined she had never heard the name of Mahomet, because I foolishly conjectured this book had been locked up for ages in the library, and was utterly unknown to the rest of the world.

All my desire was now to tell them the discovery I had made; for I thought, when they knew of the existence of *Mahometanism Explained*, they would read it, and become Mahometans, to ensure themselves a safe passage over the silken bridge. But it wanted more courage than I possessed to break the matter to my intended converts; I must acknowledge that I had been reading without leave; and the habit of never speaking, or being spoken to, considerably increased the difficulty.

My anxiety on this subject threw me into a fever. I was so ill that my mother thought it necessary to sleep in the same room with me. In the middle of the night I could not resist the strong desire I felt to tell her what preyed so much on my mind.

I awoke her out of a sound sleep, and begged she would be so kind as to be a Mahometan. She was very much alarmed, for she thought I was delirious, which I believe I was; for I tried to explain the reason of my request, but it was in such an incoherent manner that she could not at all comprehend what I was talking about.

The next day a physician was sent for, and he discovered, by several questions that he put to me, that I had read myself into a fever. He gave me medicines, and ordered me to be kept very quiet, and said he hoped in a few days I should be very well; but as it was a new case to him, he never having attended a little Mahometan before, if any lowness continued after he had removed the fever, he would, with my mother's permission, take me home with him to study this extraordinary case at his leisure; and added, that he could then hold a consultation with his wife, who was often very useful to him in prescribing remedies for the maladies of his younger patients.

In a few days he fetched me away. His wife was in the carriage with him. Having heard what he said about her prescriptions, I expected, between the doctor and his lady, to undergo a severe course of medicine, especially as I heard him very formally ask her advice what was good for a Mahometan fever the moment after he had handed me into the carriage. She studied a little while, and then she said, a ride to Harlow Fair would not be amiss. He said he was entirely of her opinion, because it suited him to go there to buy a horse.

During the ride they entered into conversation with me, and in answer to their questions, I was relating to them the solitary manner in which I had passed my time; how I found out the library, and what I had read in the fatal book which had so heated my imagination—when we arrived at the fair; and Ishmael, Mahomet, and the narrow bridge vanished out of my head in an instant.

Oh! what a cheerful sight it was to me to see so many happy faces assembled together, walking up and down between the rows of booths that were full of showy things; ribands, laces, toys, cakes, and sweetmeats! While the doctor was gone to buy his horse, his kind lady let me stand as long as I pleased at the booths, and gave me many things which she saw I particularly admired. My needle-case, my pin-cushion, indeed, my work-basket and all its contents, are presents which she purchased for me at this fair. After we returned home she played with me all the evening at a geographical game, which she also bought for me at this cheerful fair.

The next day she invited some young ladies of my own age to spend the day with me. She had a swing put up in the garden for us, and a room cleared of the furniture, that we might play at blindman's buff. One of the liveliest of the girls, who had taken on herself the direction of our sports, she kept to be my companion all the time I stayed with her, and every day contrived some new amusement for us.

Yet this good lady did not suffer all my time to pass in mirth and gaiety. Before I went home she explained to me very seriously the error into which I had fallen. I found that so far from *Mahometanism Explained* being a book concealed only in this library, it was well known to every person of the least information.

The Turks, she told me, were Mahometans, and that, if the leaves of my favourite book had not been torn out, I should have read that the author of it did not mean to give the fabulous stories here related as true, but only wrote it as giving a history of what the Turks, who are a very ignorant people, believe concerning the impostor Mahomet, who feigned himself to be a descendant of Ishmael. By the good offices of the physician and his lady, I was carried home at the end of a month, perfectly cured of the error into which I had fallen, and very much ashamed of having believed so many absurdities.

Emily Barton

WHEN I was a very young child, I remember residing with an uncle and aunt who live in ——shire. I think I remained there near a twelvemonth. I am ignorant of the cause of my being so long left there by my parents, who, though they were remarkably fond of me, never came to see me during all that time. As I did not know I should ever have occasion to relate the occurrences of my life, I never thought of inquiring the reason.

I am just able to recollect that when I first went there I thought it was a fine thing to live in the country, and play with my little cousins in the garden all day long; and I also recollect that I soon found that it was a very dull thing to live in the country with little cousins who have a papa and mamma in the house, while my own dear papa and mamma were in London, many miles away.

I have heard my papa observe, girls who are not well managed are a most quarrelsome race of little people. My cousins very often quarrelled with me, and then they always said, "I will go and tell my mamma, cousin Emily;" and then I used to be very disconsolate, because I had no mamma to complain to of my grievances.

My aunt always took Sophia's part because she was so young; and she never suffered me to oppose Mary or Elizabeth, because they were older than me.

The playthings were all the property of one or other of my cousins. The large dolls belonged to Mary or Elizabeth, and the pretty little wax dolls were dressed on purpose for Sophia, who always began to cry the instant I touched them. I had nothing that I could call my own but one pretty book of stories; and one day, as Sophia was endeavouring to take it from me, and I was trying to keep it, it was all torn to pieces; and my aunt would not be angry with her. She only said, Sophia was a little baby and did not know any better. My uncle promised to buy me another book, but he never remembered it. Very often when he came home in the evening he used to say, "I wonder what I have got in my pocket;" and then they all crowded round him, and I used to creep towards him, and think, maybe it is my book that my uncle has got in his pocket. But, no; nothing ever came out for me. Yet the first sight of a plaything, even if it be not ones own, is always a cheerful thing, and a new toy would put them in a good humour for a while, and they would say, "Here, Emily, look what I have got. You may take it in your own hand and look at it." But the pleasure of examining it was sure to be stopped in a short time by the old story of "Give that to me again; you know that is mine." Nobody could help, I think, being a little out of humour if they were always served so; but if I showed any signs of discontent, my aunt always told my uncle I was a little peevish fretful thing, and gave her more trouble than all her own children put together. My aunt would often say, what a happy thing it was to have such affectionate children as hers were. She was always praising my cousins because they were affectionate; that was sure to be her word. She said I had not one atom of affection in my disposition, for that no kindness ever made the least impression on me. And she would say all this with Sophia seated on her lap, and the two eldest perhaps hanging round their papa, while I was so dull to see them taken so much notice of, and so sorry that I was not affectionate, that I did not know what to do with myself.

Then there was another complaint against me; that I was so shy before strangers. Whenever any strangers spoke to me, before I had time to think what answer I should give, Mary or Elizabeth would say, "Emily is so shy, she will never speak." Then I, thinking I was very shy, would creep into a corner of the room, and be ashamed to look up while the company stayed.

Though I often thought of my papa and mamma, by degrees the remembrance of their persons faded out of my mind. When I tried to think how they used to look, the faces of my cousins' papa and mamma only came into my mind.

One morning my uncle and aunt went abroad before breakfast, and took my cousins with them. They very often went out for whole days together and left me at home. Sometimes they said it was because they could not take so many children; and sometimes they said it was because I was so shy, it was no amusement to me to go abroad.

That morning I was very solitary indeed, for they had even taken the dog Sancho with them, and I was very fond of him. I went all about the house and garden to look for him. Nobody could tell me where Sancho was, and then I went into the front court and called, "Sancho, Sancho." An old man that worked in the garden was there, and he said Sancho was gone with his master. Oh! how sorry I was; I began to cry, for Sancho and I used to amuse ourselves for hours together when everybody was gone out. I cried till I heard the mail-coachman's horn, and then I ran to the gate to see the mail-coach go past. It stopped before our gate, and a gentleman got out, and the moment he saw me he took me in his arms, and kissed me, and said I was Emily Barton, and asked me why the tears were on my little pale cheeks; and I told him the cause of my distress. The old man asked him to walk into the house, and was going to call one of the servants; but the gentleman would not let him, and he said, "Go on with your work, I want to talk to this little girl before I go into the house." Then he sat down on a bench which was in the court, and asked me many questions and I told him all my little troubles, for he was such a good-natured looking gentleman that I prattled very freely to him. I told him all I have told you, and more, for the unkind treatment I met with was more fresh in my mind than it is now. Then he called to the old man, and desired him to fetch a post-chaise, and gave him money that he should make haste, and I never saw the old man walk so fast before. When he had been gone a little while, the gentleman said, "Will you walk with me down the road to meet the chaise, and you shall ride in it a little way along with me." I had nothing on, not even my old straw bonnet that I used to wear in the garden; but I did not mind that, and I ran by his side a good way, till we met the chaise, and the old man riding with the driver. The gentleman said, "Get down and open the door," and then he lifted me in. The old man looked in a sad fright, and said "Oh! sir, I hope you are not going to take the child away?" The gentleman threw out a small card, and bid him give that to his master, and calling to the post-boy to drive on, we lost sight of the old man in a minute.

The gentleman laughed very much and said, "We have frightened the old man, he thinks I am going to run away with you;" and I laughed, and thought it a very good joke, and he said, "So you tell me you are very shy;" and I replied, "Yes, sir, I am, before strangers." He said, "So I perceive you are," and then he laughed again, and I laughed, though I did not know why. We had such a merry ride, laughing all the way at one thing or another, till we came to a town where the chaise stopped, and he ordered some breakfast. When I got out I began to shiver a little, for it was the latter end of autumn; the leaves were falling off the trees, and the air blew very cold. Then he desired the waiter to go and order a straw hat and a little warm coat for me; and when the milliner came, he told her he had stolen a little heiress, and we were going to Gretna Green in such a hurry that the young lady had no time to put on her bonnet before she came out. The milliner said I was a pretty little heiress, and she wished us a pleasant journey. When we had breakfasted, and I was equipped in my new coat and bonnet, I jumped into the chaise again as warm and as lively as a little bird.

When it grew dark we entered a large city; the chaise began to roll over the stones, and I saw the lamps ranged along London streets.

Though we had breakfasted and dined upon the road, and I had got out of one chaise into another many times, and was now riding on in the dark, I never once considered where I was, or where I was going to. I put my head out of the chaise window, and admired those beautiful lights. I was sorry when the chaise stopped, and I could no longer look at the brilliant rows of lighted lamps.

Taken away by a stranger under a pretence of a short ride, and brought quite to London, do you not expect some perilous end of this adventure? Ah! it was my papa himself, though I did not know who he was till after he had put me into my mamma's arms, and told me how he had run away with his own little daughter. "It is your papa, my dear, that has brought you to your own home."—"This is your mamma, my love," they both exclaimed at once. Mamma cried for joy to see me, and she wept again when she heard my papa tell what a neglected child I had been at my uncle's. This he had found out, he said, by my own innocent prattle, and that he was so offended with his brother, my uncle, that he would not enter his house. And then he said what a little, happy, good child I had been all the way, and that when he found I did not know him, he would not tell me who he was, for the sake of the pleasant surprise it would be to me. It was a surprise and a happiness indeed, after living with unkind relations, all at once to know I was at home with my own dear papa and mamma.

My mamma ordered tea. Whenever I happen to like my tea very much, I always think of the delicious cup of tea mamma gave us after our journey. I think I see the urn smoking before me now, and papa wheeling the sofa round, that I might sit between them at the table.

Mamma called me Little Runaway, and said it was very well it was only papa. I told her how we frightened the old gardener, and opened my eyes to show her how he stared, and how my papa made the milliner believe we were going to Gretna Green. Mamma looked grave, and said she was almost frightened to find I had been so fearless; but I promised her another time I would not go into a post-chaise with a gentleman without asking him who he was: and then she laughed, and seemed very well satisfied.

Mamma, to my fancy, looked very handsome. She was very nicely dressed, quite like a fine lady. I held up my head, and felt very proud that I had such a papa and mamma. I thought to myself, "O dear, my cousins' papa and mamma are not to be compared to mine!"

Papa said, "What makes you bridle and simper so, Emily?" Then I told him all that was in my mind. Papa asked if I did not think him as pretty as I did mamma. I could not say much for his beauty, but I told him he was a much finer gentleman than my uncle, and that I liked him the first moment I saw him, because he looked so good-natured. He said, "Well, then, he must be content with that half praise; but he had always thought himself very handsome." "O dear!" said I, and fell a-laughing, till I spilt my tea, and mamma called me a little awkward girl.

The next morning my papa was going to the Bank to receive some money, and he took mamma and me with him, that I might have a ride through London streets. Every one that has been in London must have seen the Bank, and therefore you may imagine what an effect the fine large rooms, and the bustle and confusion of people had on me, who was grown such a little wondering rustic that the crowded streets and the fine shops alone kept me in continual admiration.

As we were returning home down Cheapside, papa said, "Emily shall take home some little books. Shall we order the coachman to the corner of St. Paul's Churchyard, or shall we go to the Juvenile Library in Skinner Street?" Mamma said she would go to Skinner Street, for she wanted to look at the new buildings there. Papa bought me seven new books, and the lady in the shop persuaded him to take more, but mamma said that was quite enough at present.

We went home by Ludgate Hill, because mamma wanted to buy something there; and while she went into a shop, papa heard me read in one of my new books, and said he was glad to find I could read so well, for I had forgot to tell him my aunt used to hear me read every day.

My papa stopped the coach opposite to St. Dunstan's Church, that I might see the great iron figures strike upon the bell, to give notice that it was a quarter of an hour past two. We waited some time that I might see this sight, but just at the moment they were striking, I happened to be looking at a toy-shop that was on the other side of the way, and unluckily missed it. Papa said, "Never mind; we will go into the toy-shop, and I dare say we shall find something that will console you for your disappointment." "Do," said mamma, "for I knew Miss Pearson, who keeps this shop, at Weymouth, when I was a little girl, not much older than Emily. Take notice of her,—she is a very intelligent old lady." Mamma made herself known to Miss Pearson, and showed me to her, but I did not much mind what they said; no more did papa—for we were busy among the toys.

A large wax-doll, a baby-house completely furnished, and several other beautiful toys, were bought for me. I sat and looked at them with an amazing deal of pleasure as we rode home—they quite filled up one side of the coach.

The joy I discovered at possessing things I could call my own, and the frequent repetition of the words *My own, my own*, gave my mamma some uneasiness. She justly feared that the cold treatment I had experienced at my uncle's had made me selfish, and therefore she invited a little girl to spend a few days with me, to see, as she has since told me, if I should not be liable to fall into the same error from which I had suffered so much at my uncle's.

As my mamma had feared, so the event proved; for I quickly adopted my cousins' selfish ideas, and gave the young lady notice that they were my own playthings, and she must not amuse herself with them any longer than I permitted her. Then presently I took occasion to begin a little quarrel with her, and said, "I have got a mamma now, Miss Frederica, as well as you, and I will go and tell her, and she will not let you play with my doll any longer than I please, because it is my own doll." And I very well remember I imitated, as nearly as I could, the haughty tone in which my cousins used to speak to me.

"Oh, fie! Emily," said my mamma; "can you be the little girl who used to be so distressed because your cousins would not let you play with their dolls? Do you not see you are doing the very same unkind thing to your playfellow that they did to you?" Then I saw as plain as could be what a naughty girl I was, and I promised not to do so any more.

A lady was sitting with mamma, and mamma said, "I believe I must pardon you this once, but I hope never to see such a thing again. This lady is Miss Frederica's mamma, and I am quite ashamed that she should be witness to your inhospitality to her daughter, particularly as she was so kind to come on purpose to invite you to a share in her *own* private box at the theatre this evening. Her carriage is waiting at the door to take us, but how can we accept of the invitation after what has happened?"

The lady begged it might all be forgotten; and mamma consented that I should go, and she said,

"But I hope, my dear Emily, when you are sitting in the playhouse, you will remember that pleasures are far more delightful when they are shared among numbers. If the whole theatre were your own, and you were sitting by yourself to see the performance, how dull it would seem to what you will find it, with so many happy faces around us, all amused with the same thing!" I hardly knew what my mamma meant, for I had never seen a play; but when I got there, after the curtain drew up, I looked up towards the galleries, and down into the pit, and into all the boxes, and then I knew what a pretty sight it was to see a number of happy faces. I was very well convinced that it would not have been half so cheerful, if the theatre had been my own, to have sat there by myself. From that time, whenever I felt inclined to be selfish, I used to remember the theatre where the mamma of the young lady I had been so rude to gave me a seat in her own box. There is nothing in the world so charming as going to a play. All the way there I was as dull and as silent as I used to be in ——shire, because I was so sorry mamma had been displeased with me. Just as the coach stopped, Miss Frederica said, "Will you be friends with me, Emily?" and I replied, "Yes, if you please, Frederica;" and we went hand-in-hand together into the house. I did not speak any more till we entered the box, but after that I was as lively as if nothing at all had happened.

I shall never forget how delighted I was at the first sight of the house. My little friend and I were placed together in the front, while our mammas retired to the back part of the box to chat by themselves, for they had been so kind as to come very early, that I might look about me before the performance began.

Frederica had been very often at a play. She was very useful in telling me what everything was. She made me observe how the common people were coming bustling down the benches in the galleries, as if they were afraid they should lose their places. She told me what a crowd these poor people had to go through before they got into the house. Then she showed me how leisurely they all came into the pit, and looked about them before they took their seats. She gave me a charming description of the king and queen at the play, and showed me where they sat, and told me how the princesses were dressed. It was a pretty sight to see the remainder of the candles lighted; and so it was to see the musicians come up from under the stage. I admired the music very much, and I asked if that was the play. Frederica laughed at my ignorance, and then she told me, when the play began the green curtain would draw up to the sound of soft music and I should hear a lady, dressed in black, say,

"Music hath charms to soothe the savage breast;"

and those were the very first words the actress, whose

name was Almeria, spoke. When the curtain began to draw up, and I saw the bottom of her black petticoat, and heard the soft music, what an agitation I was in! But before that we had long to wait. Frederica told me we should wait till all the dress-boxes were full, and then the lights would pop up under the orchestra; the second music would play, and then the play would begin.

This play was the Mourning Bride. It was a very moving tragedy; and after that, when the curtain dropped, and I thought it was all over, I saw the most diverting pantomime that ever was seen. I made a strange blunder the next day, for I told papa that Almeria was married to Harlequin at last; but I assure you I meant to say Columbine, for I knew very well that Almeria was married to Alphonso; for she said she was in the first scene. She thought he was dead, but she found him again, just as I did my papa and mamma, when she least expected it.

Maria Howe

I WAS brought up in the country. From my
infancy I was always a weak and tender-spirited
girl, subject to fears and depressions. My
parents, and particularly my mother, were of a very
different disposition. They were what is usually
called gay: they loved pleasure, and parties, and
visiting; but as they found the turn of my mind to be
quite opposite, they gave themselves little trouble
about me, but upon such occasions generally left
me to my choice, which was much oftener to stay at
home and indulge myself in my solitude, than to join
in their rambling visits. I was always fond of being
alone, yet always in a manner afraid. There was a
book closet which led into my mother's dressing-
room. Here I was eternally fond of being shut up
by myself, to take down whatever volumes I pleased,
and pore upon them, no matter whether they were
fit for my years or no, or whether I understood
them. Here, when the weather would not permit
my going into the dark walk, *my walk*, as it was
called, in the garden; here, when my parents have
been from home, I have stayed for hours together,
till the loneliness which pleased me so at first, has at

length become quite frightful and I have rushed out
of the closet into the inhabited parts of the house, and
sought refuge in the lap of some one of the female
servants, or of my aunt, who would say, seeing me
look pale, that Maria had been frightening herself
with some of those *nasty books:* so she used to call my
favourite volumes, which I would not have parted
with, no, not with one of the least of them, if I had
had the choice to be made a fine princess, and to
govern the world. But my aunt was no reader.
She used to excuse herself, and say that reading hurt
her eyes. I have been naughty enough to think that
this was only an excuse, for I found that my aunt's
weak eyes did not prevent her from poring ten
hours a day upon her prayer-book, or her favourite
Thomas à Kempis. But this was always her excuse for
not reading any of the books I recommended. My
aunt was my father's sister. She had never been
married. My father was a good deal older than my
mother, and my aunt was ten years older than my
father. As I was often left at home with her, and as
my serious disposition so well agreed with hers, an
intimacy grew up between the old lady and me, and
she would often say that she loved only one person in
the world and that was me. Not that she and my
parents were on very bad terms; but the old lady did
not feel herself respected enough. The attention and
fondness which she showed to me, conscious as I was
that I was almost the only being she felt anything

like fondness to, made me love her, as it was natural; indeed, I am ashamed to say, that I fear I almost loved her better than both my parents put together. But there was an oddness, a silence about my aunt, which was never interrupted but by her occasional expressions of love to me, that made me stand in fear of her. An odd look from under her spectacles would sometimes scare me away when I had been peering up in her face to make her kiss me. Then she had a way of muttering to herself, which, though it was good words and religious words that she was mumbling, somehow I did not like. My weak spirits, and the fears I was subject to, always made me afraid of any personal singularity or oddness in any one. I am ashamed, ladies, to lay open so many particulars of our family; but indeed it is necessary to the understanding of what I am going to tell you, of a very great weakness, if not wickedness, which I was guilty of towards my aunt. But I must return to my studies, and tell you what books I found in the closet, and what reading I chiefly admired. There was a great *Book of Martyrs* in which I used to read, or rather I used to spell out meanings; for I was too ignorant to make out many words; but there it was written all about those good men who chose to be burned alive rather than forsake their religion and become naughty Papists. Some words I could make out, some I could not; but I made out enough to fill my little head with vanity, and I used to think I was so courageous I could be burned too, and I would put my hands upon the flames which were pictured in the pretty pictures which the book had, and feel them; but you know, ladies, there is a great difference between the flames in a picture and a real fire, and I am now ashamed of the conceit which I had of my own courage, and think how poor a martyr I should have made in those days. Then there was a book not so big; but it had pictures in it; it was called Culpepper's *Herbal;* it was full of pictures of plants and herbs, but I did not much care for that. Then there was Salmon's *Modern History*, out of which I picked a good deal. It had pictures of Chinese gods, and the great hooded serpent, which ran strangely in my fancy. There were some law books too, but the old English frightened me from reading them. But above all, what I relished was Stackhouse's *History of the Bible*, where there was the picture of the ark, and all the beasts getting into it. This delighted me, because it puzzled me, and many an aching head have I got with poring into it, and contriving how it might be built, with such and such rooms to hold all the world if there should be another flood, and sometimes settling what pretty beasts should be saved and what should not, for I would have no ugly or deformed beast in my pretty ark. But this was only a piece of folly and vanity that a little reflection might cure me of. Foolish girl that I was! to suppose that any creature is really ugly that has all its limbs contrived with heavenly wisdom, and was doubtless formed to some beautiful end, though a child cannot comprehend it. Doubtless a frog or a toad is not uglier in itself than a squirrel or a pretty green lizard; but we want understanding to see it.

(*Here I must remind you, my dear Miss Howe, that one of the young ladies smiled and two or three were seen to titter at this part of your narration, and you seemed, I thought, a little too angry for a girl of your sense and reading; but you will remember, my dear, that young heads are not always able to bear strange and unusual assertions; and if some elder person, possibly, or some book which you had found, had not put it into your head, you would hardly have discovered by your own reflection that a frog or a toad was equal in real loveliness to a frisking squirrel, or a pretty green lizard, as you called it; not remembering that at this very time you gave the lizard the name of pretty, and left it out to the frog—so liable we are all to prejudices. But you went on with your story*).

These fancies, ladies, were not so very foolish or naughty, perhaps, but they may be forgiven in a child of six years old; but what I am going to tell, I shall be ashamed of, and repent, I hope, as long as I live. It will teach me not to form rash judgments. Besides the picture of the ark, and many others which I have forgot, Stackhouse contained one picture which made more impression upon my childish understanding than all the rest. It was the picture of the raising up of

Samuel, which I used to call the Witch of Endor picture. I was always very fond of picking up stories about witches. There was a book called *Glanvil on Witches*, which used to lie about in this closet; it was thumbed about, and showed it had been much read in former times. This was my treasure. Here I used to pick out the strangest stories. My not being able to read them very well probably made them appear more strange and out of the way to me. But I could collect enough to understand that witches were old women who gave themselves up to do mischief—how by the help of spirits as bad as themselves they lamed cattle, and made the corn not grow; and how they made images of wax to stand for people that had done them any injury, or they thought had done them injury; and how they burned the images before a slow fire, and stuck pins in them; and the persons which these waxen images represented, however far distant, felt all the pains and torments in good earnest, which were inflicted in show upon these images; and such a horror I had of these wicked witches, that though I am now better instructed, and look upon all these stories as mere idle tales, and invented to fill people's heads with nonsense, yet I cannot recall to mind the horrors which I then felt without shuddering, and feeling something of the old fit return.

(*Here, my dear Miss Howe, you may remember that Miss M——, the youngest of our party, showing some*

*more curiosity than usual, I winked upon you to hasten
to your story, lest the terrors which you were describing
should make too much impression upon a young head, and
you kindly understood my sign, and said less upon the
subject of your fears than I fancy you first intended).*

This foolish book of witch stories had no pictures
in it, but I made up for them out of my own fancy,
and out of the great picture of the raising of Samuel
in Stackhouse. I was not old enough to understand
the difference there was between these silly improbable tales, which imputed such powers to poor old
women, who are the most helpless things in the
creation, and the narrative in the Bible, which does
not say that the witch, or pretended witch, raised up
the dead body of Samuel by her own power; but, as
it clearly appears, he was permitted by the divine will
to appear to confound the presumption of Saul; and
that the witch herself was really as much frightened
and confounded at the miracle as Saul himself, not
expecting a real appearance; but probably having
prepared some juggling, sleight-of-hand tricks and
sham appearance to deceive the eyes of Saul: where-
as she, nor any one living, had never the power to
raise the dead to life, but only He who made them
from the first. These reasons I might have read in
Stackhouse itself if I had been old enough, and have
read them in that very book since I was older, but at
that time I looked at little beyond the picture.

These stories of witches so terrified me, that my

sleeps were broken, and in my dreams I always had a
fancy of a witch being in the room with me. I know
now that it was only nervousness; but though I can
laugh at it now as well as you, ladies, if you knew
what I suffered, you would be thankful that you have
had sensible people about you to instruct you and
teach you better. I was let grow up wild like an ill
weed, and thrived accordingly. One night that I
had been terrified in my sleep with my imaginations,
I got out of bed and crept softly to the adjoining
room. My room was next to where my aunt usually
sat when she was alone. Into her room I crept for
relief from my fears. The old lady was not yet
retired to rest, but was sitting with her eyes half-open
half-closed; her spectacles tottering upon her nose;
her head nodding over her prayer-book; her lips
mumbling the words as she read them, or half-read
them in her dozing posture; her grotesque appearance; her old-fashioned dress, resembling what I had
seen in that fatal picture in Stackhouse; all this, with
the dead time of night, as it seemed to me (for I had
gone through my first sleep), joined to produce a
wicked fancy in me, that the form which I had beheld
was not my aunt, but some witch. Her mumbling
of her prayers confirmed me in this shocking idea.
I had read in Glanvil of those wicked creatures
reading their prayers *backwards*, and I thought that
this was the operation which her lips were at this
time employed about. Instead of flying to her

friendly lap for that protection which I had so often experienced when I have been weak and timid, I shrunk back terrified and bewildered to my bed, where I lay in broken sleeps and miserable fancies till the morning, which I had so much reason to wish for, came. My fancies a little wore away with the light, but an impression was fixed, which could not for a long time be done away. In the daytime, when my father and mother were about the house, when I saw them familiarly speak to my aunt, my fears all vanished; and when the good creature has taken me upon her knees and shown me any kindness more than ordinary, at such times I have melted into tears and longed to tell her what naughty foolish fancies I had had of her. But when night returned, that figure which I had seen recurred—the posture, the half-closed eyes, the mumbling and muttering which I had heard—a confusion was in my head, *who* it was I had seen that night:—it was my aunt, and it was not my aunt:—it was that good creature, who loved me above all the world, engaged at her good task of devotions—perhaps praying for some good to me. Again, it was a witch—a creature hateful to God and man, reading backwards the good prayers; who would perhaps destroy me. In these conflicts of mind I passed several weeks, till, by a revolution in my fate, I was removed to the house of a female relation of my mother's, in a distant part of the country, who had come on a visit to our house, and observing my lonely ways, and apprehensive of the ill effect of my mode of living upon my health, begged leave to take me home to her house to reside for a short time. I went with some reluctance at leaving my closet, my dark walk, and even my aunt, who had been such a source of both love and terror to me. But I went, and soon found the grand effects of a change of scene. Instead of melancholy closets and lonely avenues of trees, I saw lightsome rooms and cheerful faces; I had companions of my own age; no books were allowed me but what were rational and sprightly; that gave me mirth or gave me instruction. I soon learned to laugh at witch stories; and when I returned after three or four months, absence to our own house, my good aunt appeared to me in the same light in which I had viewed her from my infancy, before that foolish fancy possessed me, or rather, I should say, more kind, more fond, more loving than before. It is impossible to say how much good that lady, the kind relation of my mother's that I spoke of, did to me by changing the scene. Quite a new turn of ideas was given to me; I became sociable and companionable; my parents soon discovered a change in me, and I have found a similar alteration in them. They have been plainly more fond of me since that change, as from that time I learned to conform myself more to their way of living. I have never since had that aversion to company and going out with them which used to make them regard me with less fondness than they would have wished to show. I impute almost all that I had to complain of in their neglect to my having been a little, unsociable, uncompanionable mortal. I lived in this manner for a year or two, passing my time between our house and the lady's who so kindly took me in hand, till, by her advice, I was sent to this school;—where I have told you, ladies, what for fear of ridicule I never ventured to tell any person besides, the story of my foolish and naughty fancy.

Charlotte Wilmot

THE MERCHANT'S DAUGHTER

UNTIL I was eleven years of age my life was one continued series of indulgence and delight. My father was a merchant, and supposed to be in very opulent circumstances, at least I thought so, for at a very early age I perceived that we lived in a more expensive way than any of my father's friends did. It was not the pride of birth, of which, Miss Withers, you once imagined you might justly boast, but the mere display of wealth that I was early taught to set an undue value on. My parents spared no cost for masters to instruct me; I had a French governess, and also a woman-servant whose sole business it was to attend on me. My playroom was crowded with toys, and my dress was the admiration of all my youthful visitors, to whom I gave balls and entertainments as often as I pleased. I looked down on all my young companions as my inferiors; but I chiefly assumed airs of superiority over Maria Hartley, whose father was a clerk in my father's counting-house, and therefore I concluded she would regard the fine show I made with more envy and admiration than any other of my companions. In the days of my humiliation, which I too soon experienced, I was thrown on the bounty of her father for support. To be a dependant on the charity of her family seemed the heaviest evil that could have befallen me; for I remembered how often I had displayed my finery and my expensive ornaments, on purpose to enjoy the triumph of my superior advantages; and, with shame I now speak it, I have often glanced at her plain linen frock, when I showed her my beautiful ball-dresses. Nay, I once gave her a hint, which she so well understood that she burst into tears, that I could not invite her to some of my parties because her mamma once sent her on my birthday in a coloured frock. I cannot now think of my want of feeling without excessive pain; but one day I saw her highly amused with some curious toys, and on her expressing the pleasure the sight of them gave her, I said, "Yes, they are very well for those who are accustomed to these things; but, for my part, I have so many, I am tired of them, and I am quite delighted to pass an hour in the empty closet your mamma allows you to receive your visitors in, because there is nothing there to interrupt the conversation."

Once, as I have said, Maria was betrayed into tears; now that I insulted her by calling her own small apartment an empty closet, she turned quick on me, but not in anger, say, "Oh, my dear Miss Wilmot, how very sorry I am"——Here she stopped; and though I knew not the meaning of her words, I felt it as a reproof. I hung down my head abashed; yet perceiving that she was all that day more kind and obliging than ever, and being conscious of not having merited this kindness, I thought she was mean-spirited, and therefore I consoled myself with having discovered this fault in her, for I thought my arrogance was full as excusable as her meanness.

In a few days I knew my error; I learned why Maria had been so kind, and why she had said she was sorry. It was for me, proud disdainful girl that I was, that she was sorry; she knew, though I did not, that my father was on the brink of ruin; and it came to pass, as she feared it would, that in a few days my playroom was as empty as Maria's closet, and all my grandeur was at an end.

My father had what is called an execution in the house, everything was seized that we possessed. Our splendid furniture, and even our wearing apparel, all my beautiful ball-dresses, my trinkets, and my toys, were taken away by my father's merciless creditors. The week in which this happened was such a scene of hurry, confusion, and misery, that I will not attempt to describe it.

At the end of a week I found that my father and mother had gone out very early in the morning. Mr. Hartley took me home to his own house, and I expected to find them there; but, oh! what anguish did I feel, when I heard him tell Mrs. Hartley they had quitted England, and that he had brought me home to live with them. In tears and sullen silence I passed the first day of my entrance into this despised house. Maria was from home. All the day I sat in a corner of the room grieving for the departure of my parents; and if for a moment I forgot that sorrow, I tormented myself with imagining the many ways which Maria might invent to make me feel in return the slights and airs of superiority which I had given myself over her. Her mother began the prelude to what I expected, for I heard her freely censure the imprudence of my parents. She spoke in whispers; yet, though I could not hear every word, I made out the tenor of her discourse. She was very anxious, lest her husband should be involved in the ruin of our house. He was the chief clerk in my father's counting-house. Towards evening he came in and quieted her fears by the welcome news that he had obtained a more lucrative situation than the one he had lost.

At eight in the evening Mrs. Hartley said to me, "Miss Wilmot, it is time for you to be in bed, my dear;" and ordered the servant to show me upstairs, adding that she supposed she must assist me to undress, but that when Maria came home, she must teach me to wait on myself. The apartment in which I was to sleep was at the top of the house. The walls were white-washed, and the roof was sloping. There was only one window in the room, a small casement, through which the bright moon shone, and it seemed to me the most melancholy sight I had ever beheld. In broken and disturbed slumbers I passed the night. When I awoke in the morning, she whom I most dreaded to see, Maria who I supposed had envied my former state, and who I now felt certain would exult over my present mortifying reverse of fortune, stood by my bedside. She awakened me from a dream, in which I thought she was ordering me to fetch her something; and on my refusal, she said I must obey her, for I was now her servant. Far differently from what my dreams had pictured did Maria address me! She said in the gentlest tone imaginable, "My dear Miss Wilmot, my mother begs you will come down to breakfast; will you give me leave to dress you?" My proud heart would not suffer me to speak, and I began to attempt to put on my clothes; but never having been used to do anything for myself, I was unable to perform it, and was obliged to accept of the assistance of Maria. She dressed me, washed my face, and combed my hair; and as she did these services for me, she said in a most respectful manner, "Is this the way you like to wear this, Miss Wilmot?" or, "Is this the way you like this done?" and courtesied as she gave me every fresh article to put on. The slights I expected to receive from Maria would not have distressed me more than the delicacy of her behaviour did. I hung down my head with shame and anguish.

In a few days Mrs. Hartley ordered her daughter to instruct me in such useful works and employments as Maria knew. Of everything which she called useful I was most ignorant. My accomplishments I found were held in small estimation here, by all indeed, except Maria. She taught me nothing without the kindest apologies for being obliged to teach me, who, she said, was so excellent in all elegant arts; and was for ever thanking me for the pleasure she had formerly received from my skill in music and pretty fancy works. The distress I was in made these complimentary speeches not flatteries, but sweet drops of comfort to my degraded heart, almost broken with misfortune and remorse.

I remained at Mr. Hartley's but two months; for at the end of that time my father inherited a considerable property by the death of a distant relation, which has enabled him to settle his affairs. He established himself again as a merchant; but as he wished to retrench his expenses, and begin the world again on a plan of strict economy, he sent me to this school to finish my education.

Susan Yates

I WAS born and brought up in a house in which
my parents had all their lives resided, which
stood in the midst of that lonely tract of land
called the Lincolnshire Fens. Few families besides
our own lived near the spot, both because it was
reckoned an unwholesome air, and because its
distance from any town or market made it an in-
convenient situation. My father was in no very
affluent circumstances, and it was a sad necessity
which he was put to of having to go many miles to
fetch anything from the nearest village, which was
full seven miles distant, through a sad miry way that
at all times made it heavy walking, and after rain was
almost impassable. But he had no horse or carriage
of his own.

The church which belonged to the parish in which
our house was situated stood in this village; and its
distance being, as I said before, seven miles from our
house made it quite an impossible thing for my
mother or me to think of going to it. Sometimes,
indeed, on a fine dry Sunday my father would rise
early, and take a walk to the village, just to see how
goodness thrived, as he used to say; but he would generally

return tired, and the worse for his walk. It is scarcely possible to explain to any one who has not lived in the Fens what difficult and dangerous walking it is. A mile is as good as four, I have heard my father say, in those parts. My mother, who in the early part of her life had lived in a more civilised spot, and had been used to constant church-going, would often lament her situation. It was from her I early imbibed a great curiosity and anxiety to see that thing which I had heard her call a church, and so often lament that she could never go to. I had seen houses of various structures, and had seen in pictures the shapes of ships and boats, and palaces and temples, but never rightly anything that could be called a church, or that could satisfy me about its form. Sometimes I thought it must be like a house, and sometimes I fancied it must be more like the house of our neighbour, Mr. Sutton, which was bigger and handsomer than ours. Sometimes I thought it was a great hollow cave, such as I have heard my father say the first inhabitants of the earth dwelt in. Then I thought it was like a waggon, or a cart, and that it must be something movable. The shape of it ran in my mind strangely, and one day I ventured to ask my mother what was that foolish thing she was always longing to go to, and which she called a church. Was it anything to eat or drink, or was it only like a great huge plaything to be seen and stared at?—I was not quite five years of age when I made this inquiry.

This question, so oddly put, made my mother smile; but in a little time she put on a more grave look, and informed me that a church was nothing that I had supposed it, but it was a great building, far greater than any house which I had seen, where men and women and children came together twice a day on Sundays, to hear the Bible read, and make good resolutions for the week to come. She told me that the fine music which we sometimes heard in the air came from the bells of St. Mary's Church, and that we never heard it but when the wind was in a particular point. This raised my wonder more than all the rest; for I had somehow conceived that the noise which I heard was occasioned by birds up in the air, or that it was made by the angels, whom (so ignorant I was till that time) I had always considered to be a sort of birds; for before this time I was totally ignorant of anything like religion, it being a principle of my father that young heads should not be told too many things at once, for fear they should get confused ideas and no clear notions of anything. We had always indeed so far observed Sundays, that no work was done upon that day, and upon that day I wore my best muslin frock, and was not allowed to sing or to be noisy; but I never understood why that day should differ from any other. We had no public meetings: indeed, the few straggling houses which were near us would have furnished but a slender congregation; and the loneliness of the place we lived in, instead of making us more sociable, and drawing us closer together, as my mother used to say it ought to have done, seemed to have the effect of making us more distant and averse to society than other people. One or two good neighbours indeed we had, but not in numbers to give me an idea of church attendance.

But now my mother thought it high time to give me some clearer instruction in the main points of religion, and my father came readily into her plan. I was now permitted to sit up half an hour later on a Sunday evening that I might hear a portion of Scripture read, which had always been their custom, though by reason of my tender age, and my father's opinion on the impropriety of children being taught too young, I had never till now been an auditor. I was taught my prayers, and those things which you, ladies, I doubt not, had the benefit of being instructed in at a much earlier age.

The clearer my notions on these points became, they only made me more passionately long for the privilege of joining in that social service, from which it seemed that we alone, of all the inhabitants of the land, were debarred; and when the wind was in that point which enabled the sound of the distant bells of St. Mary's to be heard over the great moor which skirted our house, I have stood out in the air to catch the sounds, which I almost devoured; and the tears have come into my eyes when sometimes they seemed to speak to me almost in articulate sounds, to *come to church*, and because of the great moor which was between me and them, I could not come; and the too tender apprehensions of these things have filled me with a religious melancholy. With thoughts like these I entered into my seventh year.

And now the time was come when the great moor was no longer to separate me from the object of my wishes and of my curiosity. My father having some money left him by the will of a deceased relation, we ventured to set up a sort of a carriage—no very superb one, I assure you, ladies; but in that part of the world it was looked upon with some envy by our poorer neighbours. The first party of pleasure which my father proposed to take in it was to the village where I had so often wished to go, and my mother and I were to accompany him; for it was very fit, my father observed, that little Susan should go to church and learn how to behave herself, for we might some time or other have occasion to live in London, and not always be confined to that out-of-the-way spot.

It was on a Sunday morning that we set out, my little heart beating with almost breathless expectation. The day was fine, and the roads as good as they ever are in those parts. I was so happy and so proud! I was lost in dreams of what I was going to see. At length the tall steeple of St. Mary's Church came in view. It was pointed out to me by my father, as the place from which that music had come, which I had heard over the moor, and had fancied to be angels singing. I was wound up to the highest pitch of delight at having visibly presented to me the spot from which had proceeded that unknown friendly music; and when it began to peal, just as we approached the village, it seemed to speak, *Susan is come*, as plainly as it used to invite me *to come*, when I heard it over the moor. I pass over our alighting at the house of a relation, and all that passed till I went with my father and mother to church.

St. Mary's Church is a great church for such a small village as it stands in. My father said it had been a cathedral, and that it had once belonged to a monastery, but the monks were all gone. Over the door there was stonework, representing saints and bishops, and here and there, along the sides of the church, there were figures of men's heads made in a strange grotesque way: I have since seen the same sort of figures in the round tower of the Temple Church in London. My father said they were very improper ornaments for such a place, and so I now think them; but it seems the people who built these great churches in old times gave themselves more liberties than they do now; and I remember that when I first saw them, and before my father had made this observation, though they were so ugly and out of shape, and some of them seem to be grinning and distorting their features with pain or with laughter, yet being placed upon a church, to which I had come with such serious thoughts, I could not help thinking they had some serious meaning; and I looked at them with wonder, but without any temptation to laugh. I somehow fancied they were the representation of wicked people set up as a warning.

When we got into the church, the service was not begun, and my father kindly took me round to show me the monuments and everything else remarkable. I remember seeing one of a venerable figure, which my father said had been a judge. The figure was kneeling, as if it was alive, before a sort of desk, with a book, I suppose the Bible, lying on it. I somehow fancied the figure had a sort of life in it, it seemed so natural, or that the dead judge that it was done for said his prayers at it still. This was a silly notion, but I was very young, and had passed my little life in a remote place, where I had never seen anything nor knew anything; and the awe which I felt at first being in a church took from me all power but that of wondering. I did not reason about anything; I was too young. Now I understand why monuments are put up for the dead, and why the figures which are put upon them are described as doing the actions which they did in their lifetimes, and that they are a sort of pictures set up for our instruction. But all was new and surprising to me on that day—the long windows with little panes, the pillars, the pews made of oak, the little hassocks for the people to kneel on, the form of the pulpit, with the sounding-board over it, gracefully carved in flower-work. To you, who have lived all your lives in populous places, and have been taken to church from the earliest time you can remember, my admiration of these things must appear strangely ignorant. But I was a lonely young creature, that had been brought up in remote places, where there was neither church nor church-going inhabitants. I have since lived in great towns, and seen the ways of churches and of worship, and I am old enough now to distinguish between what is essential in religion, and what is merely formal or ornamental.

When my father had done pointing out to me the things most worthy of notice about the church, the service was almost ready to begin; the parishioners had most of them entered and taken their seats; and we were shown into a pew where my mother was already seated. Soon after the clergyman entered and the organ began to play what is called the voluntary. I had never seen so many people assembled before. At first I thought that all eyes were upon me, and that because I was a stranger. I was terribly ashamed and confused at first; but my mother helped me to find out the places in the prayer-book, and being busy about that took off some of my painful apprehensions. I was no

stranger to the order of the service, having often read
in the prayer-book at home, but my thoughts being
confused, it puzzled me a little to find out the re-
sponses and other things, which I thought I knew so
well; but I went through it tolerably well. One
thing which has often troubled me since is, that I am
afraid I was too full of myself and of thinking how
happy I was, and what a privilege it was for one that
was so young to join in the service with so many
grown people, so that I did not attend enough to the
instruction which I might have received. I remember I foolishly applied everything that was said to
myself, so as it could mean nobody but myself, I was
so full of my own thoughts. All that assembly of
people seemed to me as if they were come together
only to show me the way of a church. Not but I
received some very affecting impressions from some
things which I heard that day; but the standing up
and sitting down of the people, the organ, the singing:—the way of all these things took up more of my
attention than was proper; or I thought it did. I
believe I behaved better, and was more serious when
I went a second time, and a third time; for now we
went as a regular thing every Sunday, and continued
to do so, till, by a still further change for the better in
my father's circumstances, we removed to London.
Oh! it was a happy day for me my first going to St.
Mary's Church; before that day I used to feel like a
little outcast in the wilderness, like one that did not

belong to the world of Christian people. I have never felt like a little outcast since. But I never can hear the sweet noise of bells, that I don't think of the angels singing, and what poor but pretty thoughts I had of angels in my uninstructed solitude.

Arabella Hardy

I WAS born in the East Indies. I lost my father and mother young. At the age of five my relations thought it proper that I should be sent to England for my education. I was to be intrusted to the care of a young woman who had a character for great humanity and discretion; but just as I had taken leave of my friends, and we were about to take our passage, the young woman suddenly fell sick, and could not go on board. In this unpleasant emergency no one knew how to act. The ship was at the very point of sailing, and it was the last which was to sail for the season. At length the captain, who was known to my friends, prevailed upon my relation, who had come with us to see us embark, to leave the young woman on shore, and to let me embark separately. There was no possibility of getting any other female attendant for me in the short time allotted for our preparation; and the opportunity of going by that ship was thought too valuable to be lost. No other ladies happened to be going, and so I was consigned to the care of the captain and his crew—rough and unaccustomed attendants for a young creature delicately brought up as I had been; but indeed they did their best to make me not feel the difference. The unpolished sailors were my nursery-maids and my waiting-women. Everything was done by the captain and the men to accommodate me, and make me easy. I had a little room made out of the cabin, which was to be considered as my room, and nobody might enter into it. The first mate had a great character for bravery and all sailor-like accomplishments; but with all this he had a gentleness of manners, and a pale feminine cast of face, from ill health and a weakly constitution, which subjected him to some ridicule from the officers, and caused him to be named Betsy. He did not much like the appellation, but he submitted to it the better, saying that those who gave him a woman's name well knew that he had a man's heart, and that in the face of danger he would go as far as any man. To this young man, whose real name was Charles Atkinson, by a lucky thought of the captain, the care of me was especially intrusted. Betsy was proud of his charge, and, to do him justice, acquitted himself with great diligence and adroitness through the whole of the voyage. From the beginning I had somehow looked upon Betsy as a woman, hearing him so spoken of, and this reconciled me in some measure to the want of a maid which I had been used to. But I was a manageable girl at all times, and gave nobody much trouble.

I have not knowledge enough to give an account of

my voyage, or to remember the names of the seas we passed through, or the lands which we touched upon in our course. The chief thing I can remember (for I do not recollect the events of the voyage in any order) was Atkinson taking me upon the deck to see the great whales playing about in the sea. There was one great whale came bounding up out of the sea, and then he would dive into it again, and then would come up at a distance where nobody expected him, and another whale was following after him. Atkinson said they were at play, and that the lesser whale loved the bigger whale, and kept it company all through the wide seas; but I thought it strange play, and a frightful kind of love; for I every minute expected they would come up to our ship and toss it. But Atkinson said a whale was a gentle creature, and it was a sort of sea-elephant, and that the most powerful creatures in nature are always the least hurtful. And he told me how men went out to take these whales, and stuck long pointed darts into them; and how the sea was discoloured with the blood of these poor whales for many miles' distance; and I admired the courage of the men, but I was sorry for the inoffensive whale. Many other pretty sights he used to show me, when he was not on watch, or doing some duty for the ship. No one was more attentive to his duty than he; but at such times as he had leisure he would show me all pretty sea-sights:— the dolphins and porpoises that came before a storm, and all the colours which the sea changed to; how sometimes it was a deep blue and then a deep green, and sometimes it would seem all on fire, all these various appearances he would show me, and attempt to explain the reason of them to me, as well as my young capacity would admit of. There were a lion and a tiger on board, going to England as a present to the king; and it was a great diversion to Atkinson and me, after I got rid of my first terrors, to see the ways of these beasts in their dens, and how venturous the sailors were in putting their hands through the grates, and patting their rough coats. Some of the men had monkeys, which ran loose about, and the sport was for the men to lose them and find them again. The monkeys would run up the shrouds, and pass from rope to rope, with ten times greater alacrity than the most experienced sailor could follow them; and sometimes they would hide themselves in the most unthought-of places, and when they were found, they would grin and make mouths, as if they had sense. Atkinson described to me the ways of these little animals in their native woods, for he had seen them. Oh, how many ways he thought of to amuse me in that long voyage!

Sometimes he would describe to me the odd shapes and varieties of fishes that were in the sea, and tell me tales of sea-monsters that lay hid at the bottom, and were seldom seen by men; and what a glorious sight it would be, if our eyes could be sharpened to behold all the inhabitants of the sea at once swimming in the great deeps, as plain as we see the gold and silver fish in a bowl of glass. With such notions he enlarged my infant capacity to take in many things.

When in foul weather I have been terrified at the motion of the vessel, as it rocked backwards and forwards, he would still my fears, and tell me that I used to be rocked so once in a cradle, and that the sea was God's bed, and the ship our cradle, and we were as safe in that greater motion as when we felt that lesser one in our little wooden sleeping-places. When the wind was up, and sang through the sails, and disturbed me with its violent clamours he would call it music, and bid me hark to the sea-organ, and with that name he quieted my tender apprehensions. When I have looked around with a mournful face at seeing all *men* about me, he would enter into my thoughts, and tell me pretty stories of his mother and his sisters, and a female cousin that he loved better than his sisters, whom he called Jenny, and say that when we got to England I should go and see them, and how fond Jenny would be of his little daughter, as he called me; and with these images of women and females which he raised in my fancy, he quieted me for a while. One time, and never but once, he told me that Jenny had promised to be his wife if ever he came to England, but that he had his doubts whether he should live to get home, for he was very sickly. This made me cry bitterly.

That I dwell so long upon the attention of this Atkinson, is only because his death, which happened just before we got to England, affected me so much, that he alone of all the ship's crew has engrossed my mind ever since; though indeed the captain and all were singularly kind to me, and strove to make up for my uneasy and unnatural situation. The boatswain would pipe for my diversion, and the sailor-boy would climb the dangerous mast for my sport. The rough foremastman would never willingly appear before me till he had combed his long black hair smooth and sleek, not to terrify me. The officers got up a sort of play for my amusement, and Atkinson, or, as they called him, Betsy, acted as the heroine of the piece. All ways that could be contrived were thought upon to reconcile me to my lot. I was the universal favourite; I do not know how deservedly; but I suppose it was because I was alone, and there was no female in the ship besides me. Had I come over with female relations or attendants, I should have excited no particular curiosity; I should have required no uncommon attentions. I was one little woman among a crew of men; and I believe the homage which I have read that men universally pay to women, was in this case directed to me in the absence of all other womenkind. I do not know how that might be, but I was a little princess among them, and I was not six years old.

I remember the first drawback which happened to

my comfort was Atkinson's not appearing the whole of one day. The captain tried to reconcile me to it by saying that Mr. Atkinson was confined to his cabin; that he was not quite well, but a day or two would restore him. I begged to be taken in to see him, but this was not granted. A day, and then another came, and another, and no Atkinson was visible, and I saw apparent solicitude in the faces of all the officers, who nevertheless strove to put on their best countenances before me, and to be more than usually kind to me. At length, by the desire of Atkinson himself, as I have since learned, I was permitted to go into his cabin and see him. He was sitting up, apparently in a state of great exhaustion; but his face lighted up when he saw me, and he kissed me and told me that he was going a great voyage, far longer than that which we had passed together, and he should never come back; and though I was so young, I understood well enough that he meant this of his death, and I cried sadly; but he comforted me, and told me that I must be his little executrix, and perform his last will, and bear his last words to his mother and his sisters, and to his cousin Jenny, whom I should see in a short time; and he gave me his blessing, as a father would bless his child, and he sent a last kiss by me to all his female relations, and he made me promise that I would go and see them when I got to England. And soon after this he died. But I was in another part of the ship when he died, and I was not told it till we got to shore, which was a few days after; but they kept telling me that he was better and better, and that I should soon see him but that it disturbed him to talk with any one. Oh, what a grief it was when I learned that I had lost an old shipmate that had made an irksome situation so bearable by his kind assiduities; and to think that he was gone, and I could never repay him for his kindness!

When I had been a year and a half in England, the captain, who had made another voyage to India and back, thinking that time had alleviated a little the sorrow of Atkinson's relations, prevailed upon my friends who had the care of me in England to let him introduce me to Atkinson's mother and sisters. Jenny was no more; she had died in the interval, and I never saw her. Grief for his death had brought on a consumption, of which she lingered about a twelvemonth and then expired. But in the mother and the sisters of this excellent young man I have found the most valuable friends I possess on this side the great ocean. They received me from the captain as the little *protégée* of Atkinson, and from them I have learned passages of his former life; and this in particular, that the illness of which he died was brought on by a wound of which he never quite recovered, which he got in the desperate attempt, when he was quite a boy, to defend his captain against a superior force of the enemy which had boarded him, and which, by his premature valour inspiriting the men, they finally succeeded in repulsing. This was that Atkinson who, from his pale and feminine appearance, was called Betsy; this was he whose womanly care of me got him the name of a woman; who, with more than female attention, condescended to play the handmaid to a little unaccompanied orphan that fortune had cast upon the care of a rough sea-captain and his rougher crew.

THE END